306090 03

09|02

BG EA SU NG GA YO CC AW MG

Alexander F Briseno

Jonathan D Solomon

Editors and Publishers

Emily Abruzzo

Andrew Yang

Editors

Melissa Gronlund

Cara Soh

Associate Editors

John Wagner

Design Consultant

M. Christine Boyer   Mario Gandelsonas   David L Hays   Mark Jarzombeck   Paul Lewis   Michael Sorkin

COVER EDITORIAL TEXT LAYOUT PROOFING PRINTER

306090 is an independent architectural journal published and distributed semi-annually. 306090 seeks to publish diverse, inquisitive projects by students and young professionals that have not been published elsewhere.

Opinions expressed in 306090 are the author's alone and do not necessarily reflect those of the editors.

Distributed By:
Princeton Architectural Press
37 East Seventh Street
New York, NY 10003
1.800.722.6657
www.papress.com

Contact publisher for Library of Congress Cataloging-in-Publication Data

www.306090.org   info@306090.org

306090, Inc. is a non-profit institution registered in the state of New Jersey. Your donations are tax deductible. For information on how to contribute or for ordering information please contact us at: info@306090.org or visit our Website.

05 04 03 02 5 4 3 2 1 First Edition
ISBN 1-56898-384-0

ADVISORY BOARD

URBAN EDUCATION

What *is* an urban education? Students in cities and suburbs across the world may have any number of answers to that, but we know well enough that an urban education does not rely on location in an urban area, rather it is one that engages the *urbis*; one that exists within the context not of a discourse but of a community, large or small. An urban education relies on the social context of a community, regardless of its proximity to a major metropolis.

In this, the third issue of 306090, we explore the various types of design and design education that integrate—even allow for—the existence of social context. The projects in issue three range from the direct and aggressive community interaction sponsored by Archeworks in Chicago, to the formal manifestations of energy politics in California as tackled by Yusuke Obuchi, to a low-cost tent community for relief workers as proposed by Ottawa-based Bakery Group. In short, the definition of socially conscious design is broad, and the options for working in a socially conscious manner produce varied projects across the geographic and ideological spectrum.

This variety is encouraging. It bespeaks a movement, a shift, a manifesto, fermenting within the discipline as a whole. We have determined that in order to remain meaningful, architectural education must lay aside the academic treatise briefly, and become reacquainted with the more aggressive political positioning of the manifesto. Architectural education must encourage students to take a position—social, political, academic, environmental, the list goes

306090 03 09 | 02

pp. 6-7 "Urban Education" ©2002 Alexander Briseno and Jonathan Solomon, Published by 306090, Inc.

on—with their work. 306090 dedicates itself to publishing projects and articles of an aggressive and controversial nature. From the brazen "Case for Good Design" prepared by students at Archeworks, to the subtle inversion of developer-driven construction techniques explored by su11, these projects activate their context because they take a position: that architecture can help people, that it can be something to understand, want and need.

The notion that Architecture can serve a community rather than drain it may come as a shock to the younger generations. In glossy media and in our academic institutions, where amnesia too often still reigns, design is portrayed as the style of form, or the fashion of genius. In the work of Rem Koolhaas, possibly the most significant influence on students of architecture over the past decade, design is $2,000 per square-foot luxury retail, while Lagos burns.

At a time when the very need for Architecture is itself being questioned, when most of the building done in America is executed without an architect, the projects published here demonstrate uncommon bravery for standing up and saying:
"We need Architecture!"

A hope for Architecture's social conscience glimmers.

This is issue three.

The Editors

SYSTEMATIC

su11

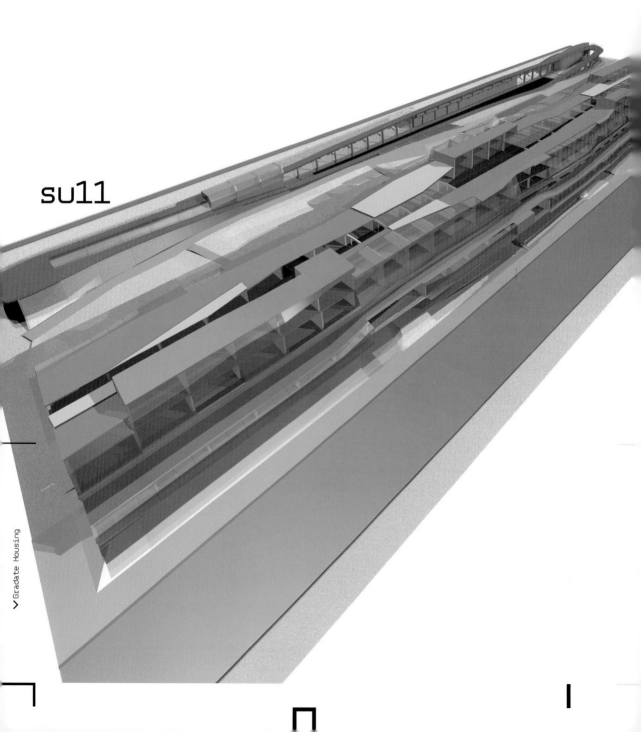

˅Gradate Housing

su11 designs environments that are catching up to the way we live

VARIATIONS

by Eva Pankenier

306090 03 09 | 02

Published by 306090, Inc.

pp. 08-19 "Systematic Variations" ©2002 su11 and Eva Pankenier,

What happens when architecture is organized not by tradition but by a programmatic understanding based on current lifestyle models?

This is a question that has inspired architects since the Modernist movement, but in spite of the last few decades' increasing incorporation of technological innovation into our lives, our built environment has not kept pace. Enter the work of the young firm su11, which was started in 1998 as a partnership between Ferda Kolatan and Erich Schoenenberger, who are driven by this very question. Su11 consistently explores what happens when we fully embrace a technological lifestyle. In projects ranging in scale from a computer station and office cubicle to a small "mobile" home and a community complex, the design process begins with analyses of live/ work models and realistic lifestyle diagrams, and ends in a user-driven design with the architect's role slightly recast. In their work, the architect is a guide and interpreter, rather than dictator of "good" design.

The projects shown on these pages at first glance appear form-driven (and visually reminiscent of recent work by Neil Denari and Foreign Office), but that take is misleading. In both the Gradate Housing and Composite Housing projects, as well as the POD/Office, the tenant/buyer either selects freely, over time perhaps, from a kit of parts, or selects the optimal programmatic prototype that closest

su11 has been published in Archilab's Futurehouse, +81, Surface, Interior Design, Arch+, Monitor Magazine, Deutsche Bauzeitung, LA Times, Washington Post, Le Monde, V.S.D., route Actualite, Building Design, Totem Magazine, Beaux Arts Magazine, Men's Journal, New York, NOVA 1 *and* Viewpoint Magazine.

su11 have participated in exhibitions worldwide, including: ART Basel, ICFF, Archilab 2001 and Housing for the Next 10 Million.

They have won numerous awards, including the 2001 Swiss National Culture Award for Art and Design and ICFF Editors Award for New Designer.

Ferda Kolatan received his Architectural Diploma from the RWTH Aachen in 1993 and his Master of Architecture at Columbia University in 1995. Before starting su11, Kolatan was a Senior Designer for Smith-Miller + Hawkinson Architects. He also taught Design Studios at Columbia and was a visiting professor at the University of British Columbia. Currently he is an Adjunct Professor at Rennselear Polytechnic Institute, New York.

Erich Schoenenberger received his Bachelor of Environmental Design at the Technical School of Nova Scotia in 1993 and his Master of Architecture at Columbia University in 1995. He has worked for Santiago Calatrava and as a Senior Designer at Kol/Mac Studio in New York. He has taught digital design courses at Columbia. Kolatan and Schoenenberger founded su11 architecture+design in 1998.

www.su11.com

Eva Pankenier received her Master of Architecture from the Royal Institute of Technology in Stockholm and her Bachelor of Arts in Architecture from LeHigh University. She lives in Sweden.

resembles their style of living and/or working. The personalized elements are then incorporated into a generalized structural framework that expresses the overall vision of the architect. Only in the final phase does the physical form become known. The process is not sculptural, but instead born out of an additive process. The final form is a product of constant structural framework, along with variables and insertable parts.

This work bears some similarity to the work of the Office for Mobile Design, and other's engaged in similar investigations. However, the work of su11 is unique in that not only are the homes mobile, they are also completely customizable by the user and not dictated by the designer

What is surprising about the work of su11 is not that it liberates ideas and prototypes for how we live and work, but rather that it leaves design in the hands of the user. We seldom call into question the historical references and standards we incorporate into our homes. Only in extreme cases, with that rare visionary client, is the architect allowed the space to produce something truly reflective of existing cultural and technological climates.

These are alternative cutting-edge proposals that respond to our living environments—and to the lives we actually lead. Why are developers today so reluctant to conceive of such projects—is the reflection of our own lifestyles such a liability? Either nostalgia inadvertently informs most of what is designed and built today, or we are simply out of touch with how we truly live today, relying on past models for home and work. Our environments must catch up with the way we live.

Most recent residential work is not that client-driven, but arises out of conceptions about what is most marketable and most likely to attract the right tenants. In truth, urban and suburban real-estate developers rarely consult potential tenants to find out if the frameworks they produce reflect current needs or desires. Striving only for the highest common denominator, they provide nothing unique or personal, and quickly become a once-hyped part of the backdrop of mediocrity in the cityscape. As such, our homes are not often prototypes for a new current lifestyle, but rather reflect what developers think others expect. We can only make our best attempt to personalize the given backdrop. Herein lies the importance of su11's abandonment of preconceptions about how we live and work.

What Kolatan and Schoenenberger propose—at least conceptually—is to closely examine how time might be distributed among various activities to create a system that complements generality on a large scale with specificity on a small scale.

In the office system, the user is able to customize the office environment with modules that incorporate wall panels with seating, accessories, lighting and privacy screens. With material variations, the possibilities are endless. In life as in work, "we find ourselves continuously blurring the boundaries between different activities in order to achieve a more integrated lifestyle and a higher degree of efficiency" writes su11. Allowing for many possible "scenarios of overlap" becomes the aspiration of the designer — to create a system that encourages flexibility. In other words, the structural and infrastructural aspects are made more or less generic, better to receive the inserts that personalize the space.

This is the overarching idea even in su11's residential projects, with a slight modification of scale.

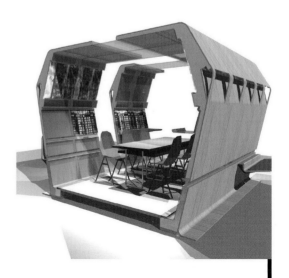

306090 03 09 | 02

POD/Office: Smart Modules for a Flexible Office Landscape

This open-ended system was designed to accommodate an ever-changing office landscape and to adapt to individual solutions and scales without losing professional integrity.

The office can be configured in many different ways providing contained spaces as well as more open and continuous conditions.

Each module offers a variety of versions, which can be combined to achieve different working and relaxational scenarios.

POD/Office: Sub_System

Once in place, the configurations can be altered, expanded and updated as needed (as pictured below).

A variety of panels create different office furniture using the same sub-structure. These panels are made out of steel, plastomeres and laminates and can be added, subtracted or changed at any time.

pp. 08-19 "Systematic Variations" ©2002 su11 and Eva Parkenier, Published by 306090, Inc.

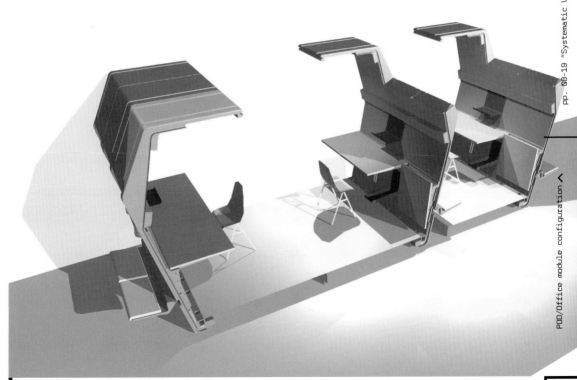

POD/Office module configuration ‹

A project like Composite Housing builds into the kit of parts concept the possibility of fast and cheap mass production. This flexible system amounts to a catalog of factory-made program parts, such as the "kitchen sink—outdoor shower—rooftop hot tub unit" and the "indoor fireplace—outdoor grill—stairs unit" which are plugged into an on-site constructed modular wooden box. The net result is a basic hub that can be varied indefinitely, added on to or reconfigured. There is "not a single moment of frozen creativity", according to Kolatan, but potentially at least, a continuous work-in-progress. Such living thus incorporates a discovery process where additional catalog parts can be ordered by catalog or Internet as the buyer's needs or means change or as new parts are introduced to the market.

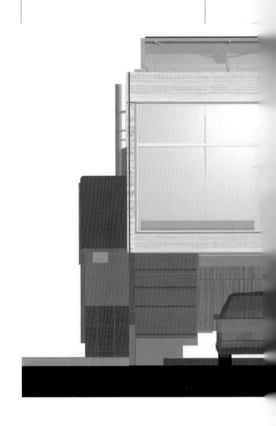

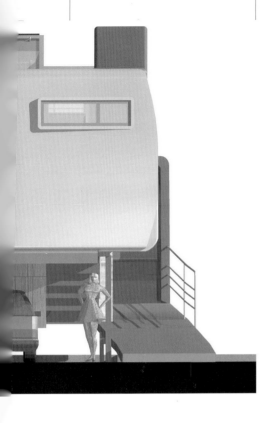

306090 03 09 | 02

pp. 08-19 "Systematic Variations" ©2002 su11 and Eva Pankenier, Published by 306090, Inc.

Composite Housing

In a time where most consumer products are marketed as pieces of individual expression rather than mere functional necessities, where "desired objects" come as singular parts within a much larger regiment of siblings, we wonder how an enhanced state of choice, progress and exchangeability could inform architectural production and its deployment.

"Composite Housing" is a twofold approach to developing new thinking towards pre-fabrication and mass-customization through new design concepts, material technologies, and a contemporary marketing strategy.

The skeleton of this single-family, free-standing house is provided by local contractors with either wood or steel, following the customary practice of the region. This allows for quick and affordable building while engaging the local community. Small varieties of shapes are given to allow for various house sizes catering to single occupants and families alike. All structures have the same incremental basis, creating a uniform template.

The second branch of this project deals with pre-fabricated "Add-On" units, which complement the on-site structure to fully functional buildings. Add-On units are conceptualized as a sort of appliance-extension. They blur the boundaries between appliance, furniture and space while creating an architectural element that defies easy categorization. Appliances are frequently updated within a household to keep up with the latest innovations. The flexibility of being able to exchange these products as the owner wishes is extended to the Add-On units and therefore impacts the program-matic and spatial configuration of his home. These units come in different variations and would be produced by third-parties to ensure a competitive market and progressive innovation.

The owner can configure his house through his personal choice of Add-On units, order them via the Web and have them delivered and installed on-site. Over the years he may update them to satisfy his taste or to accommodate a different programmatic concept.

There is a definite reference to the trailer home in
the scale of the final structure due to the practical,
low-income nature that both the typical trailer home
and su11's Composite Housing share. By bringing
the low-tech part of the construction process to the
site (the wood frame is simple and generic enough
that virtually any local crew could erect it), su11
strives to provide assistance to local construction
crews. The hi-tech plug-ins themselves use innovative materials, such as form-pressed laminates or
molded fiberglass and are more spatial concentra-
tions of functions than built-ins; essentially, hybrids
of furniture and appliance. Inevitably, however, the
final configuration of plug-ins creates interior and
exterior combinations that define the space inside
and out. The final form and character of the resulting
composite is left not up to the designer, but to the
design sense of the user.

Kolatan and Schoenenberger are quick to point out
that they do not see their task as designers to "con-
tain a program." In fact, they avoid the word "room"
on their drawings, allowing one (possible) function to
define a space instead, such as "sleep" or "eating."
Presumably, this encourages a certain freedom to
inhabit a space, either formally or informally, for other
functions in the lifetime of the home. While this is an
innovative concept today, it was in fact true for much
architecture before the 20th century, when a kitchen
just happened to be the room in which cooking was
done, where working, sleeping and eating were done
where there was space.

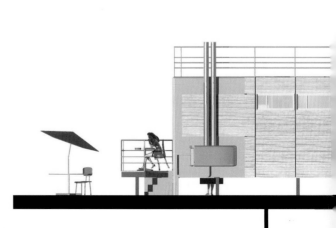

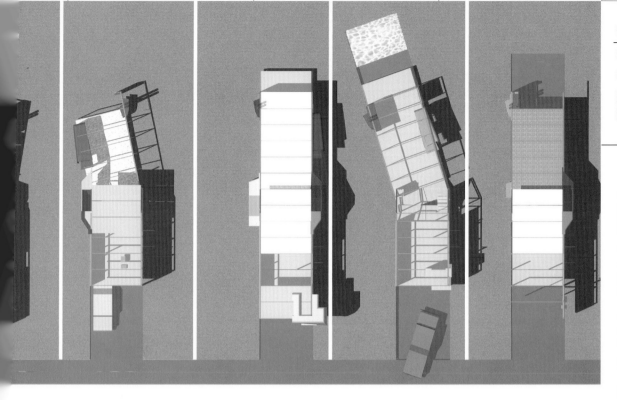

306090   03   09 | 02

pp. 08-19 "Systematic Variations" ©2002 sull and Eva Parkenier, Published by 306090, Inc.

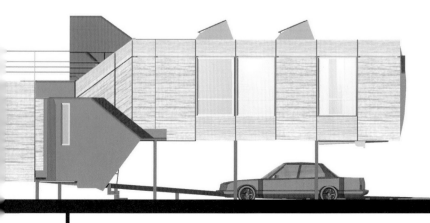

Composite Housing elevation ⌃

A project like Gradate Housing would theoretically proceed as follows: the architect, after collecting interested parties, would assist the client in isolating their own needs and selecting the appropriate living type. The choices are limited, so once the client has made a selection, the designer assembles these parts into a framework that integrates them within the structure and common recreational and shared spaces. The assembled parts are neither random nor pre-arranged, although the designer guides the additive process. As such, the final form is not ideally extended ad infinitum, rather it has an inherent point of completion. Formalistically, the ends taper, the gradating spine has a beginning and an end. That is not to say, however, that flexibility is not incorporated into the model, since the mediating corridor provides the variable in the equation. Here, a buffer zone is created that not only provides circulation space, but also acts as a display area or as a semipublic storefront.

The communal aspect of the final product is clear. There is a thoughtfulness in the work that aspires to promote the way we live today with a consciousness that we are social beings, living mostly within urban or suburban organisms. Gradate Housing is not a hotel of private refuges, but an interactive conglomeration, requiring from the residents some degree of intellectualism and interaction with each other as they utilize the shared resources that would presumably make such a living arrangement desirable in the first place. Beyond the standard-fare gym and laundry room in the basement, Gradate Housing offers the opportunity for a tenant to arrange a client-meeting by reserving one of the shared conference rooms or to arrange an exhibit in the Mediating Corridor as a way of marketing their work.

Su11's recent work promotes a designer-role that demonstrates the possibility of navigating a territory between the generic, programmatically limited apartment types constructed today and the completely blank canvas of a loft warehouse space. The appeal lies equally in the flexibility of reintegrating living and working spaces as well as in the infusion of social consciousness with design. Incorporating new material technology, such as molded fiberglass and laminates, frees the designer from constraints of material precedent, which further encourages reinvention of program. Smooth, rounded shapes and continuous surfaces make transitions between functions gradual, allowing for the "in-between conditions that may encourage unusual appropriation," in the words of su11. Such a model reflects the contemporary lifestyle model of interwoven lives of domesticity, professionalism and leisure that we all aspire to lead.

306090 03 09 | 02

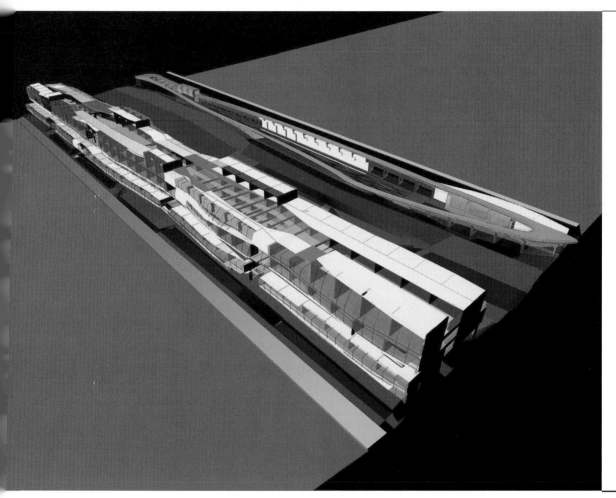

pp. 08-19 "Systematic Variations" ©2002 su11 and Eva Pankenier. Published by 306090, Inc.

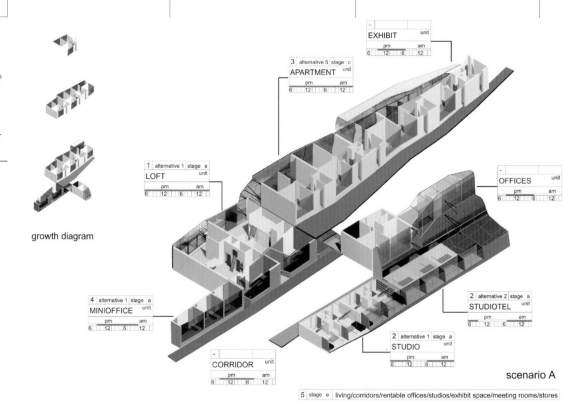

growth diagram

EXHIBIT — unit
6 | 12 | 6 | 12

3 alternative 5 stage c
APARTMENT unit
pm am
6 | 12 | 6 | 12

1 alternative 1 stage a
LOFT unit
pm am
6 | 12 | 6 | 12

OFFICES — unit
pm am
6 | 12 | 6 | 12

4 alternative 1 stage a
MINIOFFICE unit
pm am
6 | 12 | 6 | 12

2 alternative 2 stage a
STUDIOTEL unit
pm am
6 | 12 | 6 | 12

2 alternative 1 stage a
STUDIO unit
pm am
6 | 12 | 6 | 12

CORRIDOR — unit
pm am
6 | 12 | 6 | 12

scenario A

5 | stage e | living/corridors/rentable offices/studios/exhibit space/meeting rooms/stores

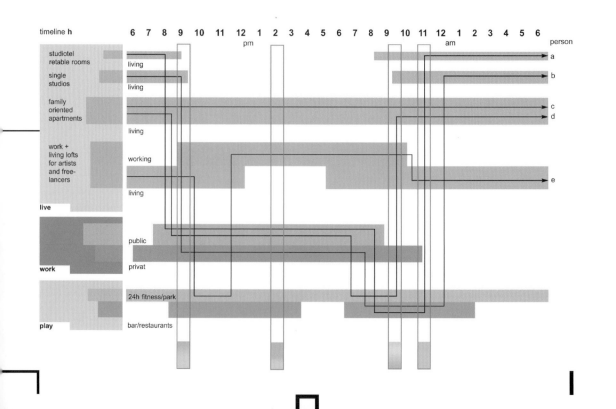

timeline h   6 7 8 9 10 11 12 1 2 3 4 5 6 7 8 9 10 11 12 1 2 3 4 5 6   person
                              pm   am

studiotel
retable rooms   living   a

single
studios   living   b

family
oriented   c
apartments   d
                     living

work +
living lofts   working
for artists
and free-
lancers   living   e

live

                     public
work
                     privat

                     24h fitness/park
play
                     bar/restaurants

Gradate housing

The structure of everyday life has become increasingly complex and virtually impossible to describe in determined categories such as 'home', 'work' or 'leisure'. These terms may form one's daily routine, yet the boundaries between them are blurry and will continue this trend in the future.

Individual lives seek individual solutions. Flexibility in terms of personal schedule and immediate accessibility of required and desired programs define one's 'life-style' and should be reflected in their homes.

Home today needs to incorporate these other programs in order to provide the widest possible ground on which inhabitants may have the chance to engage on multiple levels at various times. Work space and living space grow together since the electronic progress encourages work and speedy communication systems allow exchange over long distances without actual travel.

Leisure, entertainment and recreation activities are much more integrated in everyone's life as they used to be in the past. In-between-activities fill up the remaining blank spots on our calendars and need to be conveniently accessible. The freedom of individual planning extends the time frame further in which additional programs may be adapted. This project deals these issues by providing utmost flexibility in adapting to varied programs over time. (24 hours as well as 365 days)

Different housing types, such as studios, lofts and apartments are configured by the users' schedule and combined in a way that allows maximum transformation. Not only are the insides of the units flexible, the corridors of the building become vacant in-between spaces ready for utilization by dominating programs. (Mediating Corridor)

The growth and shape of the whole building is also determined by the most progressive, programmatic applications. The term "Gradate Housing" describes how the "intermediate" becomes the guiding infrastructure for this project. The spaces shift through different grades of program, over time, without freezing at a certain condition.

A living space, which becomes a working space , and then becomes a leisure space becomes a display space. One neighbor's work becomes the other neighbor's entertainment. Pocket spaces function as filter between grades of private and public life.

Parts of the building prosper and grow, others stand still and may transform into something else. The habitant's activities define the building shape. And vice versa, the building's layouts enable the habitants to combine and coordinate their activities.

306090 03 09 | 02

pp. 08-19 "Systematic Variations" ©2002 su11 and Eva Pankenier, Published by 306090, Inc.

Gradate Housing timeline cross-section

AIR TRANSPARENT

Normal Group for Architecture

306090 03 09 | 02

Weiss and von Fischer re-interpret a modernist obsession and see it clearer than Mies could ever have hoped

by Andrew Yang

Srdjan Janovic Weiss and Sabine Von Fischer, Normal Group for Architecture, have created projects that travel along the theoretical progression of transparency. A favorite modernist obsession, the notion of transparency is manifest in these projects, which embrace it, thwart it, or mischievously stage the illusion of it. Yes that's right, illusion. Into the 21st century now, and architects are still occupied with the same issues of transparency they were in the 1900s. While the rest of us can't seem to shake it, Normal Group is putting transparency in its place. The clarity (both literal and theoretical) in the work of Janovic Weiss and von Fischer adds a new layer to the manipulation of transparency in architecture.

Folded into ideas of light, lightness and clarity, the initial use of glass in modern buildings prompted transparency as a major issue in architecture. At first initiating the engagement of interior and exterior, the issue has gained a new layer. Discussing the issue of transparency in his book, *The Architectural Uncanny*, Anthony Vidler writes: "Literal transparency is of course notoriously difficult . . . to attain; it quickly turns into obscurity (its apparent apposite) and reflectivity (its reversal)." The work of Normal Group follows that more complex and nuanced idea than it does the traditional idea of transparency. Normal Group has been forging experiments in the past few years, experiments which have taken ideas beyond mere surface values. "We may begin to dis-

Normal Group for Architecture are Srdjan Jovanovic Weiss and Sabine von Fischer. Since its founding in 1998, Normal Group worked in architectural design and research and exhibited and lectured at Museum fur Gestaltung, Zürich, TN Probe-Tokyo, Cooper Union, University of Texas in Austin, ETH-Zürich, and Museum of Applied Arts in Belgrade. In November 2002, Normal Group will have a solo-exhibition at the Museum of Architecture, at the Serbian Academy of Arts and Sciences, Belgrade.

Sabine von Fischer graduated at ETH-Zürich, Switzerland [Dipl. Arch. ETH] where she was awarded exchange studies at RISD in Providence and Harvard GSD in Cambridge, MA, and currently studies at Columbia University. She worked with Angelil/Graham architects, Schnebli-Ammann-Ruchat architects and Althammer + Hochuli in Zürich. In New York, she worked with Anderson Architects and Sage Wimer Coombe. She is currently a partner in Normal Group for Architecture. She teaches design at ETH-Zürich, writes for architectural press and is a contributor to Cabinet magazine for Art and Culture.

Srdjan Jovanovic Weiss graduated at Faculty of Architecture, University of Belgrade [Dipl.Ing.Arh] and at Harvard University [M.Arch.II II]. He worked within various architectural groups in Belgrade and since 1997 with Richard Gluckman/GMA, Robert Wilson, director and with Jenny Holzer, artist, and researched with Rem Koolhaas [Harvard Guide to Shopping, Taschen]. He is currently a partner in Normal Group for Architecture. He has taught design at FAU Belgrade, Columbia University and U-Penn. He is an editor of Akcelerator [www.akcelerator.org] and a contributing editor of Cabinet magazine for Art and Culture.

www.normalgroup.net

Andrew Yang is an editor and partner of 306090.

pp. 20-29 "Air Transparent" ©2002 Normal Group for Architecture, Andrew Yang, Published by 306090, Inc.

cern the emergency of a more complex stance," continues Vidler, "one that, without rejecting the technological and ideological heritage of modernism, [but] nevertheless seeks to problematize its premises, recognizing that the 'subject' of modernity has indeed been destabilized by its worst effects." In their work, Normal Group has inherited this modernist legacy, and are imbuing their work not with the seemingly nihilistic "worst effects" of modernism, but bringing it to its more developed understanding. While their work uses transparency in a similar fashion, they see it not as a vehicle towards seeing through nothingness, but instead, they see it as a window toward bringing the subjects of both sides toward greater clarity.

dge around the pavilion blurry walls filter the actual view in 1:1 scale.

ion, another blurring wall appears. It forms the front of the building meant to serve the foundation's curatorial needs.

THE BLUR BUILDING

Meant as complimentary structure adjacent to Mies's Barcelona Pavilion, Blur was a project that won second prize in an international competition sponsored by Spanish architecture magazine *2G*. This project, which has not been built, bears a strong resemblance to Diller + Scofidio's similarly named construct. However, Normal Groups' building could not stand theoretically further from the latter.

Finally erected this past summer, Diller + Scofidio's structure is composed of pipes and other mist-giving apparatus. Floating above Lake Neuchâtel in Switzerland, the Blur Building drew acclaim for its fabulous nothingness. As critic Ned Cramer wrote in the July 2002 issue of *Architecture*, "The terror of the Blur Building, in other words, comes not just from the physical disorientation and dislocation it causes in people walking through it, but from an implication that something similar is occurring on a planetary scale." However, it has become far too easy to bring attention to the indeterminacy of modern life when it comes to such abstraction. Writing about the disappearing façade several years ago, critic Aaron Betsky also referenced Diller + Scofidio's as-yet-unbuilt project, commenting that "architecture might disappear into more than almost nothing."

Why nothing? Normal Group, in their Blur project, has brought substance to abstraction—which is a far more difficult task. Their project also stages an abstract façade, but it is not simply a "blur", some kind of floating cloud, bringing architecture towards nothingness—instead it is a structure bringing ideas toward being. Originally built in 1930, and reconstructed in the mid-1980s, the current Barcelona Pavilion is itself an illusion of a Miesian archetype-a throwback to purity, a recurring dream of the 1930s and, like an old relationship, the ex we cannot seem to get over. Normal Group's blur is in fact reflecting-both literally and metaphorically—what is already an optical and ideological illusion, as tactile and viscous as water evaporating into air. As Janovic Weiss and von Fischer wrote of their own project, "Blurring allows one to walk past the pavilion and to see it over and over again, yet to be reminded of the myth." It mirrors the vision of the pavilion, and makes its image dissolve into the body of an actual building—theirs. Though seemingly innocuous, this design takes a critical stance against abstract nothingness by staging such a condition, and collapsing it on itself. Behind the façade is very much a real building, interacting within this modern-historical context, but not enslaved to it in any way.

THREADWAXING SPACE

In the Threadwaxing Space Gallery, a renovation for an art gallery in downtown Manhattan, the experiment was not so much to design a gallery space, but more toward creating interplay between public and private functions. Integration of the exhibition spaces and office space—essentially both interior spaces permitting the function of production and the other enabling the production of the gaze—presented a unique opportunity for further exploration towards the ideas of transparency. This was accomplished through the installation of wall panels made from translucent corrugated fiberglass. While it omitted any kind of literal transparency, it invited parties on both the private and public side of these walls toward further engagement. Who was really being watched here? Could the activities of the office be observed in the same way as the observers from inside the private domain? Was it still private? The malleable interplay between these two roles can be almost obliterated in this organic tissue.

306090 03 09 | 02

pp. 20-29 "Air Transparent" ©2002 Normal Group for Architecture, Andrew Yang, Published by 306090, Inc.

∧Thread Waxing Space transparent Walls

SEVERAL TRUTHS

Normal Group began designing a stage set for "Several Truths," a performance by the Gina Gibney dance company, towards the end of the choreography process. As Jack Anderson, the *New York Times* dance critic noted, Gibney is noted for her distinctive integration of dance and stage setting. Normal Group was brought in to mitigate the performance space for the all-female troupe. Gibney wanted the background setting of the piece to dissolve into the floor, and vice versa. Through experimentation with different materials—and ultimately settling on fiberglass, the duo were able to create such an illusion, distilling in the performance a seamless integration of surfaces. They also created a chair, with corrugated fiberglass as the legs and back, with the seating material matching that of the floor. "They created a way that looked like it meshed. They really created an environment rather than a scrim," said Gibney. That element was integral to the needs of the performance piece—while bringing nothingness, the performance was suddenly imbued with great substance. "It was a piece where you really wanted to identify people and learn about them as individuals," said Gibney of her female dancers. "The neutral background made that possible."

Again, Normal Group found a way to create a condition of nothingness in order to shift it towards being. In this way, they are not perpetuating the nihilistic obsession of architecture-toward-nothingness. In their work, transparency provides an opening to gain clarity, and only then did the real work begin.

306090 03 09 | 02

306090, Inc.

Published by

pp. 20-29 "Air Transparent" ©2002 Normal Group for Architecture, Andrew Yarg,

RAMBLECITY

Janovic Weiss and von Fischer have themselves written about their work in terms of 'prototypes' and modularity, and modular transparencies. For them, the developed idea of prototype exists because they don't see their work as an end but as a means, from which to think and as a means, ultimately, to build. Nowhere is this idea more pronounced than in von Fischer's work for Steven Holl and Yehuda Safran's Columbia studio.

In Ramblecity, she defines a structure-in-parts that is mutable, according to urban characteristics. These semi-transparent structures—clad in steel panels with circular openings—act as a kind of membrane between exterior and interior. They attempt to establish a relationship between public and private, interior and exterior, much like the Threadwaxing Space renovation, but on an urban scale. "The shell of Ramblecity divides the inside from the outside, once being wall, once terrace, then roof, therefore creating a landscape of its own," writes von Fischer. While the idea of floor-as-wall-as-roof is something architects have been playing with for some time, von Fischer's experiment integrates this clearly. The shape and scale of the structures adapt to the topology of the landscape. Its closest peers are Leers Weinzapfel's chiller plant at the University of Pennsylvania, which uses this kind of corrugated, perforated steel outer shell, and Steven Holl's spongy dormitory for MIT, which adapts amorphous forms within a rigid grid. Ramblecity's modular structure replicates the kind of energy and functional translucency in an urban form. In essence, von Fischer tries to create in this project cohesiveness from modularities—from fragments—on a larger scale than the Normal Group has attempted before.

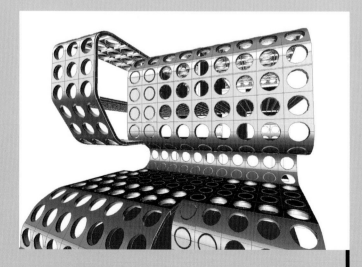

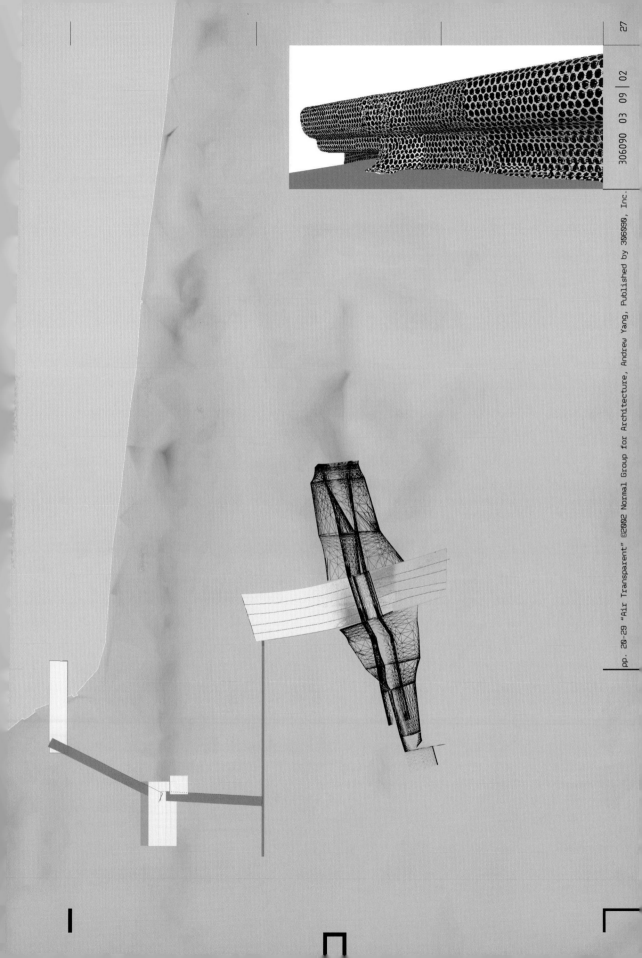

306090 03 09 02

pp. 20-29 "Air Transparent" ©2002 Normal Group for Architecture, Andrew Yang, Published by 306090, Inc.

AOMORI HOUSING PROJECT

Their most recent project, an entry for the Aomori Housing Complex competition, brings the themes of their work to its most pronounced state. This project was for an open competition that called for a housing complex in a mid-sized Japanese city which is very much urban, but still has a lasting agrarian past, on the Northern most tip of Honshu. The aim was to design a housing complex that injected some life into the urban grid, and also explored the idea of urban and rural conditions.

Very much present in the project is the idea of "Come in and be outside." Their solution to the parameters of the competition: a dense, apart-ment-style building that originates from formal but malleable shapes found in origami. Inside, above and between, are wedged rice patties. This hybrid, organic structure adapts to the formalism of the urban grid. It reflects the nature of the urban city-while not allowing it to forget the natural history from which it is born.

The development of Normal Group's interaction with transparency is brought to its most complex mani-festation here. In their submission statement, they write: "Aomori Bay and the city will appear, both in reflection and on the horizon. Walking up the ramping street, beside the rice field, to your door." It brings forward the modern obsession with transparency. In this situation, the relationship between the built and the natural condition is paramount. What's allowed to happen here is no lon-ger purely visual—the physical relationship is what's transparent.

> Amori plan + section

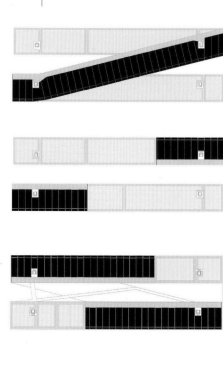
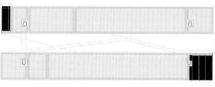
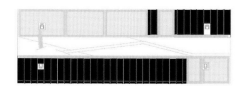
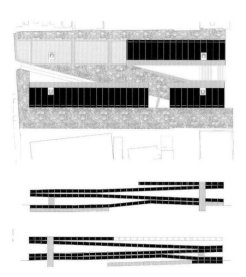

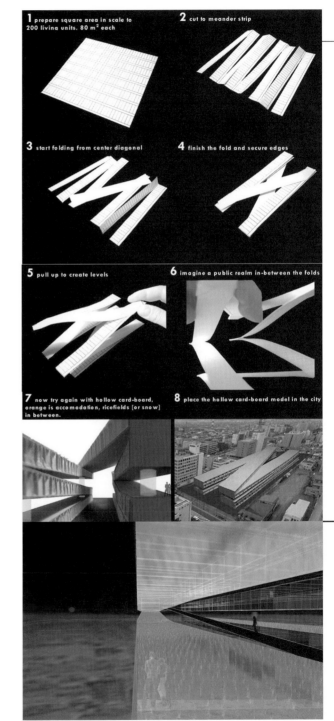

1 prepare square area in scale to 200 living units. 80 m² each

2 cut to meander strip

3 start folding from center diagonal

4 finish the fold and secure edges

5 pull up to create levels

6 imagine a public realm in-between the folds

7 now try again with hollow card-board, orange is accomodation, ricefields [or snow] in between.

8 place the hollow card-board model in the city

pp. 20-29 "Air Transparent" ©2002 Normal Group for Architecture, Andrew Yang, Published by 306090, Inc.

Origami process and perspectives <

GALLERY ANX

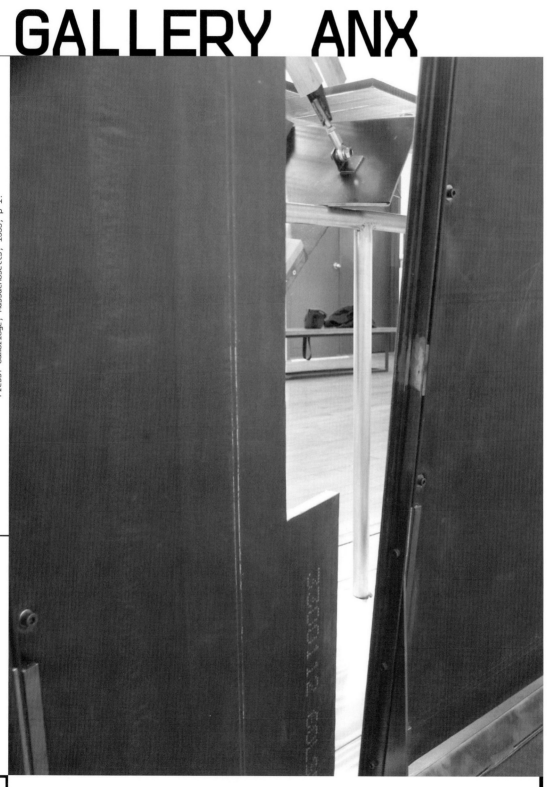

1,2. Neil Leach, The Anaesthetics of Architecture, MIT
Press: Cambridge, Massachusetts, 1999, p 1.

∨ Gallery detail

306090 03 09 | 02

pp. 30-37 "Gallery ANX" ©2002 [vent], Published by 306090, Inc.

by [vent]

Being the product of the information age, I exist in a world encapsulated by media saturation and devoid of meaning. The presentation of the image as communication has lost its essence through 'methods of visual reproduction [which] ensure[s] [our] constantly being inundated with images.[1]

—Neil Leach

This inundation of images is a result of the information age. Watch CNN and attempt to decipher the news from the advertising. Media manifests itself through the bombardment of slogans, logos and ad campaigns while corporations manipulate the latest trends, re-tooling each quarter to reflect the current cultural and strategic marketing pitches. The information society, which seemingly promotes a high level of communication, actually provides the opposite scenario. Jean Baudrillard has postulated,

> We live in a world where there is more and more information, and less and less meaning. It is precisely in this infinite cloning of the image, in this infinite proliferation of signs, that the sign itself has become invisible, the sign no longer has any meaning.[2]

[vent] was launched in 2002 as an experimental collaborative of four young designers equipped only with their ingenuity and resourcefulness. Currently spread across the country [vent] searches to define themselves as individuals while maintaining the collaboration as an evolving design entity.

[vent] began at the Kent State University School of Architecture and Environmental Design. The collaborative includes the following unique individuals, all whom received their Bachelor Architecture degrees in 2002:

Justin Gologorsky is currently employed at Wood and Zapata Architecture in Boston.

Mike Hill is currently traveling throughout the U.S.

Elizabeth Leidy resides in Boston and has most recently been employed with Thom Stauffer architects in Kent, Ohio.

Corey Yurkovich is currently employed at Freecell Architecture in Brooklyn, New York.

v_e_n_t@hotmail.com

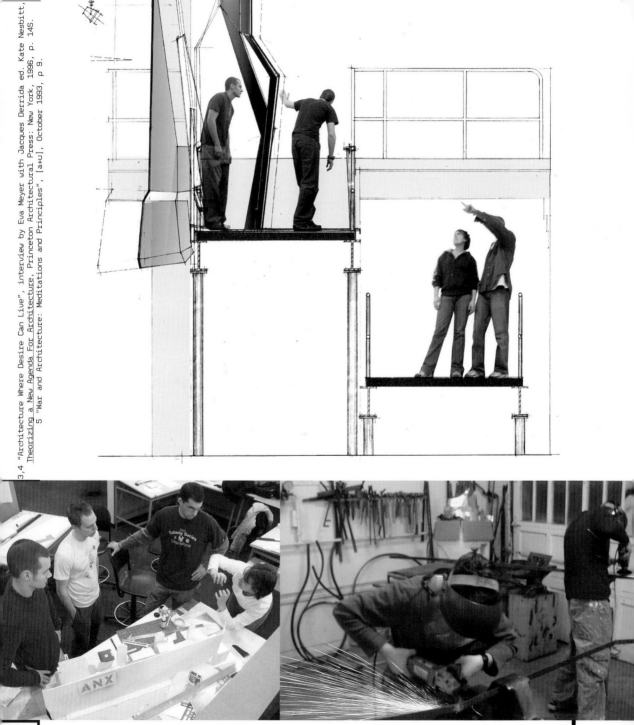

3,4 "Architecture Where Desire Can Live", interview by Eva Meyer with Jacques Derrida ed. Kate Nesbitt, Theorizing a New Agenda For Architecture, Princeton Architectural Press: New York, 1996, p. 145.
5 "War and Architecture: Meditations and Principles", [a+u], October 1993, p 9.

It is the exploitation of the image that inevitably renders everything mundane, and as citizens of this mentality of execution, we have created Gallery ANX, something out of nothing, which in the end reverts back to nothing at all.

Gallery ANX claims its title from the abbreviated scheduling label for gym annex, its primary function. It occupies an abandoned ramp system left inactive after studio renovations, and proposes to inject interest and iconography adjacent to an otherwise vast antiseptic cubicle studio environment. By exploiting the inactivity of these ramps and the multitude of variant datum elevations, the installation emphasized material as surface and frame to form an event or experience. As students, our confrontation with financial challenges molded the intention of the gallery to maximize effect through sensitive material selection and usage.

Gallery ANX is a "taking of place in space. The establishing of a place which didn't exist until then and is in keeping with what will take place there one day, that is a place."[3] Activation of the ramps came through observation and analysis of studio behaviors. With cellular phones, students gained an unprecedented connection with external parties. The development demanded what a studio environment can most often not provide: a certain intimacy in which to converse and gossip. Recognizing the pattern of retreat inspired an architecture of presentation and place to come into fruition. As Jaques Derrida states, "the bridge gathers earth as landscape around the stream . . . It does not just connect banks that are already there. The banks emerge as banks only as the bridge crosses the stream."[4] Gallery ANX acknowledges, gathers and makes visible the discovery of a ramp.

The gallery addresses the studio environment at multiple scales by re-orienting the entrance to the studios. The School of Architecture and Environmental Design began its move out of their previous building, Taylor Hall, two years ago with the creation of the annex studio for upperclassmen. It forced Taylor Hall, still occupied by the introductory studios, into a virtual ghost land. This removal of mass was made more apparent, due to lower studio's lack of juried critiques. The few alumni and local architects who were invited to engage in discussion wandered only through the annex studios, seemingly passing by Taylor Hall, never making an appearance in the obsolete building or providing the underclassmen with a much needed jury. What Gallery ANX initiated is a new approach to the studios that led past the gymnasium and directly into a glass loggia that exhibits current programs and is adjacent to the very heart of the school—its students. This proposed scenario would present the school with a street presence that is lacking on the fourth floor.

At the project's end, we asked ourselves; What does it mean to build in Cleveland? What does it mean to go to school in northeast Ohio? Cleveland's polemic is represented through the process of material consumption. Northeast Ohio is a place of manufacturing where industrial warehouse resource plants occupy the landscape. Exploiting these companies to gain product donation utilizes our marketing ingenuity. Gallery ANX is "financed from below, by those whose knowledge and ingenuity, energy and inventiveness have always fueled the heart of civilization."[5] The process of material exploration involved calling distributors and salesmen in attempts to convince them that the project would include provocative form shaping of their materials. They were curious.

306090 03 09 | 02

pp. 30–37 "Gallery ANX" ©2002 [vent], Published by 306090, Inc.

6-8 Gilles Deleuze, Foucault, ed. Sean Hand, University of Minnesota Press: Minneapolis, 1998, pp 96-99.

The outside is not a fixed limit but a moving matter animated by peristaltic movements, folds and foldings that together make up an inside: they are not something other than the outside, but precisely the inside of the outside.[6]

Gallery ANX is the investigation of four students, exploring, shaping and exposing the interior fold. "We want to undo the doubling and pull away the folds 'with a studied gesture' in order to reach the outside and its 'stifling hollowness'"[7] The exterior world, the pressures, the multitudes and the infinite crossroads of the outside act as a vast [time] continuum where "we follow the folds . . . and surround ourselves with foldings that form an 'absolute memory' in order to make the outside into a vital recurring element."[8] This element is interiority, moment, event. Gallery ANX parallels interiority—the centralized fragmented form illuminates a moment where a tensile cable network system with a corresponding undulating floor system breaks away and reveals the inside. Consciously ambiguous through form and program, clearances push the viewer to react thus they are informed how to inhabit this free space. The fragmentation creates a dichotomy of being inside yet being closely and newly oriented to the surrounding datum elevations. Being inside a system previously on the outside [above + below] forces one to re-evaluate his/her position, in reference to the physical gallery, but more importantly, to the works in the gallery.

306090 03 | 09 | 02

pp. 30-37 "Gallery ANX" ©2002 [vent], Published by 306090, Inc.

Installation at SPACES Gallery, Cleveland, OH ❯

9 War and Architecture," [a+u], October 1993, p 1.

Elevation ∨

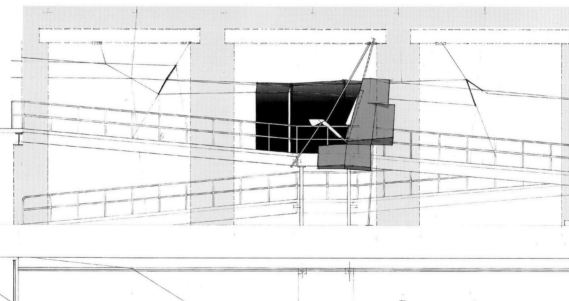

∨ Plan

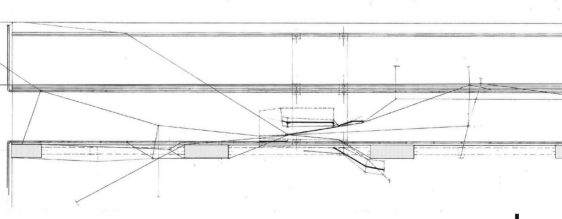

306090 03 09 | 02

The presentation of Gallery ANX in *SPACES Gallery*, an independent artist run organization on the outskirts of Cleveland fueled a transformation of our project into what people perceived to be a full-scale model or our work of art. The architecture was not able to break the formal language of object within white space. The irony of the piece is that it exists solely as a beautifully sculpted form lacking any functional role. People wanted to inhabit it but are denied. Our journey of exploitations ultimately yielded a non-architecture. As Lebbeus Woods wrote:

> I am at war with my time, with history, with all authority that resides in fixed and frightened forms.[9]

We are at war with the professionalism that exudes out of this place. The studio is a war-savaged land that requires this injection.

pp. 30-37 "Gallery ANX" ©2002 [vent], Published by 306090, Inc.

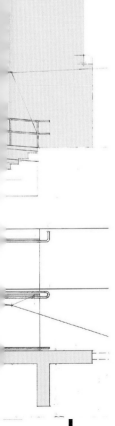

TRANSPARENCY,

306090 03 09 | 02

pp. 38–45 "Transparency, Part 2" ©2002 Emily Abruzzo, Published by 306090, Inc.

PART 2

by Emily Abruzzo

I am a sucker for good design. When I saw the item, I could not resist. Pristinely packaged in a minimal plastic Ziploc-style bag, the equally minimal book—with a CD showing though the cover—revealed artfully laid-out text, beautiful drawings and photographs, and, when extracted from its protective covering, simple yet cryptic charts and diagrams. Whatever this strange amalgam was, I had to have it. At a closer examination, the book revealed itself to be a catalog of work by the German artist collective raster-noton, presented at an event in Bern in 2000 called "taktlos-bern." The catalog, titled OACIS (Optics Acoustics Calculated in Seconds), contains reviews as well as a sampling of the group's work, which includes "sounds, images, concerts, and instal lations." This multiplicity of genres aids in the group's self-described mission, which is to respond "in a wide variety of ways to the media world in which we live."[1] Thus, the book is presented less as a tradi-tional catalog and more as a medium through which to convey experience. As written in the introduction, the "present book goes beyond the momentary, and documents stages and products in the history of this group of artists—thus adding lasting impact and enduring form to what is otherwise a transitory expe-rience."[2] Simultaneously minimal in design and mini-mal in information, the book begins to indicate an alternative body of work and approach to the dis-semination thereof. I wanted the book because the design was not only well orchestrated, but so differ-

Emily Abruzzo is partner and editor for 306090 and a Master of Architecture candidate at the School of Architecture, Princeton University. She is currently researching the intersection of fashion, retail design, and the space of the museum.

ent from other contemporary catalogs; it was the denial of flashy design and information overkill that drew me to examine raster-noton.

Raster-noton is an artist group ("a cooperation for electronic music") based in Germany, comprised of two previous artist-created "labels": rastermusic and noton.archiv für ton und michtton, which merged in 1999. The main figures of this collaboration are Olaf Bender and Frank Bretschneider (founders of rastermusic), and Carsten Nicolai (noton). Nicolai— a.k.a. Noto, a.k.a. Alva Noto, and, occasionally, a.k.a. Cyclo—has been influential in terms of the group's self-conscious image (or rather, non-image) and its concentration on the importance of design. Searching the internet for information on Nicolai, you will find his own Web page (rasternoton.de), which is, like the raster-noton page, written in all lowercase black text on a white background, with minimal information in as abbreviated form as possible.[3] The information that can be found here includes a brief statement of the groups' intent and descriptions of each of the "series" of CDs that characterizes the work of raster-noton. Also found are listings of pieces (and where they were shown, if applicable) and links to Web pages for artists whose work is disseminated by raster-noton. What is important here, however, is the very lack of information, lack of sexy graphics, lack of anything characteristic at all—unless a lacking itself can be seen as an identifying mark.

Although the work that Nicolai produces spans the realm of installation, performance, recording, and other forms, the same concept of minimal design pervades throughout. When I asked Nicolai to answer some questions about the raster-noton label via e-mail, he gladly agreed, responding in the same lowercase, abbreviated text that makes up his and the raster-noton Web sites. During our e-mail interview, he described the label as follows:

noton was founded in 1994 as a name for sound related projects, [it] was more a project name—it was supposed to describe a space—an open space, the underline [sic] of noton is: archive for sound and non sound. this polarity tries to surround the theme. the idea of the label, came later on[4]

The idea of an archive is key for Nicolai, as his work aims to collect existing material and reveal some underlying disorder through its reuse and reorganization. The sights and sounds Nicolai uses to create his work are those of modern technological residue, that is, material that is constantly being produced and changed in our developing technological world, and material that has not (commonly) been seen as artistic fodder. His sound research has led him to sample fax tones, modem hums, telephone clicks and other sounds of electronic information transmission.[5] In addition to working with material of recent phenomenon, Nicolai uses sound material that is of historical technological development, like valve amplifiers, TV tubes and waveform generators. He then edits and reproduces the material, using such techniques as interconnected video and audible loop structures created with Flash programming.

According to Armin Medosch of *Heise*, the more historical technical sounds (as described above) are favored by Nicolai, but their character (as well as that of other sounds used) becomes significantly changed when arranged into one of his compositions. Says Medosch:

Nicolai has the gift of creating minimalist soundscapes which can be of a soothing to almost healing effect to the listener. Cracking is not identical to cracking, and it is the artist's talent which brings to the fore the warmth and human-friendliness of the old electronic instruments begin used—as if the sounds of fifties electronica were a remedy to the more cruel forms of suffering which are inflicted upon us by the current software technologies.[6]

Although a certain audible friendliness may indeed be detectable due to the changed nature of the sounds used in Nicolai's work, it is probable that a first listening would prove less accessible than suggested above. Indeed, the audio loops that Nicolai creates have little to do with music in the traditional sense, and conceptually remind one more of the work of artists with minimalist aesthetics such as John Cage or Lamonte Young. The experience of listening to such works is similar: "The listener is continually pushed to reflect on the border between music and noise," affirms Will Montgomery of The Wire. He continues, "Ironic titles such as the tune-

306090 03 09 | 02

pp. 38-45 "Transparency, Part 2" ©2002 Emily Abruzzo, Published by 306090, Inc.

less 'melodie' force home the thought."[7]   This feeling that what you are listening to is "noise" or that the recorded sounds may be indistinguishable from ambient sounds points to the work of Cage. Other effects are reminiscent of Young: "At the close of his half-hour set," spoke one reviewer of a Nicolai performance, "the far-apart noises in the music suddenly thickened, clustered together and ascended to deafening volume."[8]

Unlike Cage and Young, Nicolai, while still using sounds gathered from an existing environment, reworks the sound material into a purposeful configuration (though this may not be obvious from a first listening). This follows from an intent in Nicolai's work to look for the repetitive logics inherent in the material used. The consistent use of the feedback loop aids in this mission. Nicolai is not just forcing us to listen to these sounds; he is manipulating them in order to demonstrate systemic interaction. As described in *Tema Celeste*,

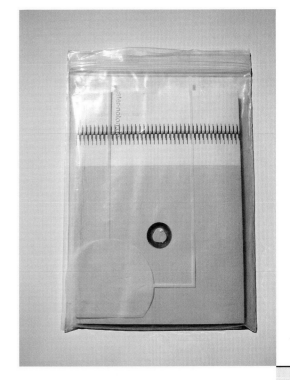

> A recurring element in his work is the attention given to cracks in the system, to deviations from a coherent internal logic, and to possible connections between different systems and languages where the focus is on the area of conflict rather than of unity.[9]

Like Young, Nicolai is attempting to reveal that which is present (yet unnoticed) in the everyday with the help of technologies. The revelation, however, happens in the realm of manipulation (not just amplification or similar techniques). What is revealed is not the sound, but something more esoteric—the mathematical structures that compose the sounds.

The sound phenomena or "structures" delineated by Nicolai's characteristic loops may be likened to architectural modernism as well. In our interview, Nicolai was sure to mention architect Buckminster Fuller as an influence, and, in fact, images of his architecture are placed throughout the OACIS book. Fuller, working with geodesic designs that allowed a complete view of the world beyond while still leaving a clear identifying mark, is an interesting figure to be seen as influential for someone working with sound. This comparison, however, allows one to understand Nicolai's intent quite clearly. Fuller, who was also interested in thought structures and looping, worked extensively with the idea of geodetics—mathematically calculated groupings and structures that form structurally "perfect" shapes. In a way, these shapes simply exist; they are found and optimized through the design process. Nicolai would likely argue that this is the exact aim of his sound pieces. In fact, critic Pinky Rose has described a "structural aural aesthetics" that could possibly be discovered by more than one electronic artist in his research.[10] This implies the mathematical patterning Nicolai tries to reveal is also universally extant, waiting to be found.

A formal concept offered by the comparison to Fuller is perhaps even more important: that of transparency, in its various forms. Fuller's geodesic domes offer a strong iconic identity while also allowing one to "see-through." It is here that the prominent non-prominence of design in the materialization and packaging of raster-noton's work clearly reflects the formal qualities present in Fuller's work—raster-noton thus artfully using a design technique to further the theoretical implications of its work.

Raster-noton being, as described by Nicolai, the vehicle via which to create, store and distribute his and other artists' work, the mode of this storage and distribution must be carefully considered in relation to the art. Very aware of this important relationship, when asked how the physical design (along with the packaging) of a raster-noton CD related to the audio content, Nicolai refused to differentiate between the two. As he wrote,

> we are interested in sound as material, so the packaging is looking to be material as well. the CD (digital storage) should have a protection system, as well as we designed [sic] different series identities, to bring more the idea of the archive to the [foreground]. raster-noton is an artist project, we as artists are involved in the [whole] process of the product, sound, mastering, design, packaging, distribution, promotion . . . all this we can decide.[11]

The "identities" Nicolai describes, however, work more like uniform non-identities. The use of transparent coverings with little or no graphics and other such techniques has allowed the raster-noton product to be compared with that of another non-design design brand, the Japanese housewares/items-for-living brand, "Muji," which translates approximately to "no label, good products." Muji products, with a similar concept of minimal design that allows a focus on function, tend to blend into the background against other household items. It is here, however, that raster-noton products have a different effect. "If Muji exploit a perceived desire to free the consumer-soul from the tyranny of corporate branding," writes Rob Young, "the raster-noton collective has a Muji-like

austerity, yet the uniqueness of the products causes them to leap out of the average CD collection."[12]

The "no-name" concept, however, is an apt comparison. In creating a strict code of alternative design, Nicolai and other members of raster-noton are attempting to eliminate the idea of artistic identity; eliminating the name-as-product amalgam that pervades the art world today. The 20' to 2000 series (as pictured) exemplifies this intent. The clear CDs, with the necessary chrome on only half of the disc, are packaged in plastic scallop cases traditionally used in the pressing plant to store the master disc. The fabrication of an almost completely transparent product (reflective where not transparent) and revelation of a hidden part of the production process has led Rob Young to call the 20' to 2000 series "the most cohesive effort to wipe out or vanish the medium." Young contends that, "Nicolai's overreaching design code for raster-noton provides the barest means for identifying the product . . . seeing through gives way to seeing beyond."[13] The idea of seeing beyond returns us to the comparison with Cage or even his contemporary Robert Rauschenberg, who gave us "blank canvases" on or through which to "see beyond." If Rauschenberg's canvases allow us to see the shadows cast and dust collected thereupon, Nicolai gives us a transparent CD case and a (partially) clear CD, through which we see the environment in which it is purchased; the environment where it is used; the machine into which it is inserted.

While the design of raster-noton's products form such a connection, the role of authorship remains a key difference between the Minimalist artists of the 60s and Nicolai. While Cage made it possible to virtually erase the author's mark from the sound composition, he often did so via a written score, which would carry his name. By contrast, Nicolai creates very specific compositions that are heavily infused with the author's influence (that, while perhaps sounding different in different spaces, have little of the infinitely varying capability that Cage's pieces have), but at the same time, puts forth this composition through the masks of a pseudonym and a label, which act to virtually erase the author's name. Nicolai does not, in fact, believe that he can be claimed as author of the physical principles that he aims to demonstrate; at the same time, Nicolai admits that "there is a conscious attempt to create distinctive styles and recognizable authors marks."[14] It is here that raster-noton's ideas on design and the way it relates to the sound material is important: it simultaneously allows for a certain anonymity (married to the use of generic, technological, cold sounds that exist in the world), and a certain identity (allowed via the directed loops and choice of sounds that are used).

306090 03 09 | 02

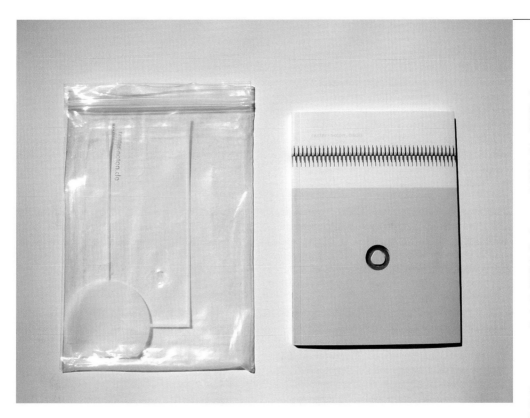

pp. 38–45 "Transparency, Part 2" ©2002 Emily Abruzzo, Published by 306090, Inc.

This complicated problem of simultaneously fading into the background and leaping out from it is fostered by an attempt to address contemporary culture quite different from that of the Minimalists. As stated by Martin Pesch, instead of reacting against the notion that art must be emotionally expressive, raster-noton:

> takes its cue from a different set of problems, namely the abundance of symbols, the symbolic nature of our everyday life (pictograms, logos, barcodes). In the face of this glut, it examines the options for individual modes of expression, for individual distinctions within the norm.[15]

The culture that this work addresses is not, then, merely the culture of pop and advertising that was so important for many artists of the 60s. It is the culture of ultimate vision; ultimate branding and monopolization; ultimate control of vision and brands by the media through which we experience it. This time, not only is television important, but the internet, the cell phone, the handheld assistant—the very items that make up the raw material of Nicolai's work. It is the searching for an individual mode of expression while retaining a (refreshing) anonymity in the face of unbridled capitalism that make the idea of the label key for raster-noton.

The label as a concept, while traditionally a capitalist structure in terms of its use in the music world, allows an unusual amount of freedom to artists using it as their mode of dissemination. In an age where technological innovations are more and more available (thus allowing the artist to take over more of the production process), the corporate label and institutional hierarchies are broken down. This allows raster-noton to be fully in control over the production and dissemination of their work, moving freely between the music and art worlds.[16]

The idea of the label as a mode of distributing an artist's work (as opposed to a gallery) not only allows certain freedoms of movement between fields. It also addresses the branding of the artist's name. The label allows for a new type of anonymity (while still retaining a certain qualitative identity) that critiques current practices of the art world. Thus, one can be sure of a certain quality level of the work, while enjoying the freedom of exploring new artists on that label. One may choose to listen to the work not because of the cover art nor the big name, but because of that which eclipses both in raster-noton series—the label (which is perversely recognized by its non-design). The notion that you no longer focus on one particular artist but, instead, on a range of work is in direct opposition to the current workings of the art world. The idea of the label, writes Susanne Binas,

> brings [raster-noton] up against the customary practices of the art world-and it is there that they realize a significant portion of their work. The art world primarily operates with big names, with the aura or image of a specific artist and his/her personal style.[17]

The focus is redirected to the label and the series, and the artist's name is subsumed by the amalgam. Nicolai's aim—to create and disseminate a body of work while eliminating the separation between composition, product (the actual artifact onto which the sound is recorded) and the design of that product—is aided by the introduction of the label.

This development of total design-integration speaks of a growing necessity in the technological world that produces the bleeps and tweaks of Nicolai's work. As we become a society where the visual surface begins to be more important than (or even replace) the physical product, this growing disunity must be considered. In his recent book, *Design and Crime*, critic Hal Foster identifies a similar need for unifying design and content in our increasingly technologically-dependant society. In an essay on the Bruce Mau book-as-visual-diarrhea model, Foster calls for the following:

a retooling of the economy around digitizing and computing, in which the product is no longer thought as an object to be produced so much as a datum to be manipulated—that is, to be designed and redesigned, consumed and reconstructed. This "mediation" also inflates design, to the point where it can no longer be considered a secondary industry. Perhaps we should speak of a "political economy of design."[18]

It is this need that Nicolai and raster-noton aim to address. The fact that Nicolai refuses to distinguish between packaging, CD and the work on the CD is evidence. Nicolai also refuses to commit his work to classification. When asked whether he sees his work as fitting into a musical or artistic tradition, he replied:

> I see myself in the tradition of complex thinking. In the moment [sic] I can find this much more in art, but this is very much up to the perception, not so much the artist [him]self.

This evasive answer, however, flies in the face of that which is so alluring about the work of raster-noton—its transparency; its obviousness. So, while the work may be a great example of Foster's "political economy of design," it is also a great example of the kind of transparency now being called for in corporations and cultural institutions alike. To quote Martin Pesch, "A raster-noton CD is a product of creativity that conjures up no illusions as to its dependence on technology." Whether revelatory of technology, finance or process, the transparency that raster-noton's work offers is appropriately timed. While the work seems at first enigmatic, it ultimately proves to hide nothing, in fact, it reveals much more than similar products (the usual CD, the usual catalog) that have been over-designed. What is revealed here, then, is the idea that with transparency comes freedom; perhaps, even, that "less" is, again, "more."

1,2 Raster-noton. OACIS [Optics Acoustics Calculated in Seconds]. Bern: 3000 Exemplare 2000
3 rasternoton.de
4 E-mail Interview, January 2002
5 Ratliff, Ben. "Music Review: Fluffs, Tremors and Skeletal Noises." New York Times. January 29, 1999: 27.
6 Medosch, Armin. "The Homeopathic Cracking Noise." Heise. April 14, 1999.
7 Montgomery, Will. "Cybernetic Dolphins." The Wire. August 2001
8 Ratliff, Ben. "Music Review: Fluffs, Tremors and Skeletal Noises." New York Times. January 29, 1999: 27.
9 Tema Celeste. No. 86 Summer 2001 http://temaceleste.com/ eng/artfeatures.asp?ID=75
10 Rose, pinky. "working models/brainmapping." OACIS [Optics Acoustics Calculated in Seconds]. Bern: 3000 Exemplare 2000, 80.
11 Interview
12 Young, Rob. "Seeing through." Oacis. 60
13 Young, Rob. "Seeing through." Oacis. 61
14 Young, Rob. "Seeing through." Oacis. 62
15 pesch, martin. "reduction. material. series. on aesthetics" Oacis 46
16 "Specific Sound" http://www.ballongmagasinet.com/ helium2/specific.html
17 Binas, Susanne. "module r-n:a portrait." Oacis. 20-21.
18 Foster, Hal. "Design and Crime." 8

306090 03 09 | 02

pp. 38-45 "Transparency, Part 2" ©2002 Emily Abruzzo, Published by 306090, Inc.

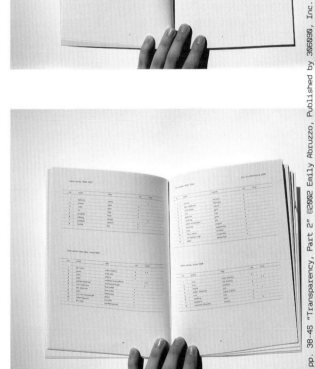

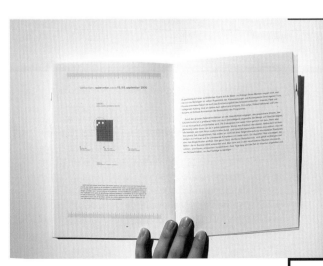

FOOD AND SHELTER

Bakery Group

v Basic Shelter

Bakery Group designs the next generation of collapsible structures for disaster aid relief

306090 03 09 | 02

by Jeff Ponitz

> We look at it as an experimental kitchen; it doesn't always taste good, but once in a while when the right ingredients are combined, well, you know . . . have you ever baked cookies?
> —Marcin Padlewski, Bakery Group

Marcin Padlewski follows a simple recipe for his design firm: use the right ingredients, and use them well. Padlewski is the director at Bakery Group, a young research and design firm in Ottawa, Canada, which has used intuitive, yet exhaustive exploration of materials in the building process to create work with economy and craft. Bakery Group's logo is an open hand, bringing to mind two notions: the act of touching and the act of building. It demonstrates their work's demand for physical interaction, both in its creation and its use. In its essence, the act of building implies taking two disparate elements and making them a unified whole. To Bakery Group, that means exploring the tangible nature of those elements, finding a common link between them, and capitalizing on that link to form a symbiotic material relationship. Be it a table that documents its own creation, a lamp that owes its origins to a wall, a tent that mimics cartilage, or a house for the homeless, each design is a record of the process that created it.

Bakery Group is based in Ottawa, Canada. The three partners, Marcin Padlewski, Anissa Szeto and Michele DuVernet all received their Bachelor of Architecture degrees from Carleton University.

Jeff Ponitz received a Bachelor of Science in Architecture from the University of Michigan. He is currently a Master of Architecture candidate at the same institution.

This text was compiled from two interviews with Bakery Group's Marcin Padlweski on 07 July 2002 and 08 July 2002; and with Anissa Szeto on 23 July 2002.

pp. 46–55 "Food and Shelter" Bakery Group and Jeff Ponitz, Published by 306090, Inc.

bakerygroup

Bakery Group takes its work both seriously and play-fully. Its lighthearted attitude can be attributed to the fact that its three members—Michele DuVernet, Anissa Szeto, and Padlewski—were all schoolmates. Padlewski and DuVernet met in primary school, and all three attended Carleton University in Ottawa. They were particularly influenced by Carleton's multi-disciplinary approach to design, where technical skills and design skills are taught as different parts of the same discipline, each relying on the other for a full understanding of design, with physical craft bringing those skills together. Material investigations of concepts remain open-ended to encourage new ideas. It is an environment that fostered building and experimentation.

Padlewski's 1997 thesis installation, "Parasite," was a product of this hands-on education. Constructed of birch plywood, MDF, steel and aluminum, the anthro-pomorphic contraption used cams and pneumatic pistons to climb up between two concrete walls. Parasite was an object without a distinct purpose other than its own existence. Padlewski enjoyed the open-ended nature of the project: "It was a free-form exploration of letting go and seeing what comes out of it; an exploration of the process of making."

With the formation of Bakery Group upon the trio's graduation, that free-form exploration has become the design ethos for the young firm. Bakery Group has found success by retaining that freedom within a set of self-imposed restraints. By focusing on material and construction, Bakery Group allows the building process to reveal new possibilities, as often through failure as through success. One of its first commissions, a simple table commissioned by Car-leton University, became a study in both. Cast of concrete, the table was to be poured on-site over a system of pin-connected supports in the floor, angled and located based on a series of calculations to most efficiently support the weight. By replacing the customary rigid panels with a vinyl sheet as the form work, the group essentially removed the only thing that would separate the concrete and the supports from each other. This allowed the struc-tural elements to interact directly and determine the table's form. Because there would only be one chance to cast the table, numerous scale models were built to predict how the concrete, vinyl, and supports would react to each other. Scale models used plaster to anticipate the concrete's behavior, and a trial run using sand instead of concrete gave them an idea of what to expect. For all this testing, however, the weight of the concrete far exceeded the predictions and, while pouring the concrete, sup-ports needed to be adjusted to compensate for forces that did not exist in scale models. In the end, the improvisational structural engineering held up; the finished product became a record of the process that created it. The supports resisted the slumping

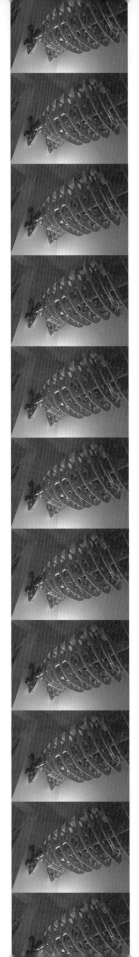

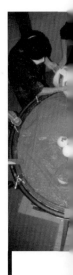

306090 03 09 | 02

pp. 46-55 "Food and Shelter" Bakery Group and Jeff Ponitz, Published by 306090, Inc.

of the concrete, which instead accumulated at the points of least resistance, farthest from the supports. This created a buoyant, tent-like form that acted as a force diagram of how the concrete and the supports react to each other. In addition, the faux-leather pattern of the vinyl was transferred to the concrete, giving it a skin-like texture to complement its graceful catenaries. Szeto calls it "a beautiful surprise." The process was full of unexpected outcomes, which, for Padlewski, points to Bakery Group's modus operandi: "When we set up a so-called program or objective, we must be open to accidents and let these demonstrate a more appropriate path, especially the destructive ones."

In such experiences, Bakery Group values the accidents that occur in the translation from concept to reality, and nowhere are they more prevalent than in the process of building. Bakery Group experimented for some time with the construction of mobile room partitions, opposing two curved translucent screens against each other to diffuse light and lend stability to the frame containing them. While the room partitions never quite caught on, Bakery Group saw potential in using the codependent structural system for lighting. Motivated by an interest in the construction process as well as a budget, it was important for them that all construction could be done by hand at home. What resulted, in 1999, was Light Volumes. The objects' frames are reduced to a single rigid panel, which is bowed and held in compression by a taught fabric skin sewn around it. Structure and skin are codependent, with tension and compression creating a graceful monolith. As in the mobile wall partition, the system lends stability to the fixture while diffusing light. The simplicity of Light Volumes gives it tremendous flexibility in function and scale: it was actually patented as a structural system, not a lighting system, and can be used as an entire wall or ceiling as easily as an accent lamp. The success of Light Volumes was so great that Italian furniture manufacturer Prandina purchased the design from Bakery Group.

Instead of viewing the Prandina transaction as profit, Bakery Group saw it as fuel for the next set of research. Their interest in lightweight, collapsible structures led them to explore an instant shelter design, suitable for a variety of applications but ideal for disaster- relief housing. Rather than dealing with the uncertainties of form first, they focused on what they wanted out of the construction. As in Light Volumes, the materials and production were to be low cost, efficient and sustainable. After looking at the tent market, they found two predominant typologies. Fully enclosed canvas structures were sturdy yet heavy, complicated and costly. Simple plastic sheet tents were cheap and lightweight, but did not offer the structure or the enclosure needed for temporary housing. Bakery Group's goal was a hybrid

of the two that provided a fully enclosed environment , and was economical because of the plastic sheet tents. An added requirement, absent from either of the two typologies, was ease and speed of deployment, essential in large-scale disaster situations. Bakery Group applied these criteria to numerous full-scale prototypes, experimenting with tonkin bamboo as a lightweight, renewable resource. They combined it with a membrane of reinforced polyethylene, the least expensive plastic specified by the United Nations High Commissioner for Refugees. While Light Volumes relied on an investigation of handcrafted production, the demands of Basic Shelter prompted the investigation and creation of a tensile structure manufacturing process taking less than three minutes per structure. To obtain this hybrid condition, they embedded the bamboo frame within the polyethylene membrane, sealing skin and structure into one symbiotic system, as in Light Volumes. "I view this system as a cartilage structure," explains Padlewski, "a skin that is dynamic and foldable until a force is applied to make it rigid."

That fusion of skin and structure gives Basic Shelter a calculated simplicity that both works well and looks good. Furthermore, the integrated structure of Basic Shelter makes it less expensive, more compact, and easier to erect than shelters currently used by relief agencies. A key feature of Basic Shelter, like Light Volumes, is its flexibility of function and scale, achieved through modularity. Each 57.8-square-foot unit can stand alone or attach to other units to form groups in configurations that vary by the given conditions. Says Szeto, "It's like a virus—it can grow in many directions and in many forms while serving many purposes." A family configuration allows for privacy spaces within four adjoined tents; a hospital scheme provides a central corridor to serve nine units; and a courtyard scheme creates a sense of community among twelve tents. The units can also form other configurations to accommodate irregular or constricting sites. The "cartilage" shell utilizes modularity as well. Interchangeable layers can be attached or removed to adapt to a range of climates: insect netting and a heat-reflecting shell for hot climates, felt or reflective insulation for cold climates.

Although the flexibility of Basic Shelter allows it to be used for a variety of different functions, it is drawing the most attention in the disaster relief market, especially after its introduction at the 2002 International Aid and Trade Exhibition in Geneva, Switzerland. While humanitarian efforts were not initially what drove Bakery Group towards Basic Shelter, Padlewski stresses the positive impact of social awareness upon design: "Our consciences are playing with us. It forces us to push our resources and push ourselves. We want to make good use of our time here." By letting that reasoning inform

306090

pp. 46-55 "Food and Shelter" Bakery Group and Jeff Ponitz, Published by 306090, Inc.

the structural and material beginnings of the project, he believes the final design finds a purpose greater than itself: "In the end, the results of that pursuit are more gratifying because they serve a basic common need; they are more real."

While a design may be completed, an idea is never exhausted. Bakery Group is using Basic Shelter to generate an assortment of related structures. By utilizing the same manufacturing process and allowing the structural system to evolve into different iterations of the original, they are creating another generation of lightweight, collapsible enclosures. A large capacity structure is being developed, and the horizontally deployed structure of Basic Shelter is being reconfigured vertically to create a wholly unique idea of what the structure can do. Bakery Group isn't sure where all the iterations will lead—they'll figure that part out later—but they are confident that they have only scratched the surface of Basic Shelter's potential.

In its work, Bakery Group fuses together skin and structure into a codependent system that upholds the individuality of each material. It makes the act of creating and the act of using into a process where each is crucial to the understanding of the object. Just as importantly, it has fused its design conscience with its social conscience so that each sensibility informs the other. Bakery Group approaches mankind's most basic needs with solutions that fit comfortably in the palm of one's hand. It does this by doing what all bakeries do: using the right ingredients, knowing how to put them together, and, well, you know. . . have you ever baked cookies?

306090 03 09 | 02

pp. 46-55 "Food and Shelter" Bakery Group and Jeff Ponitz, Published by 306090, Inc.

Thus far, Basic Shelter has been introduced at the 2002 International Aid and Trade Exhibition in Geneva. The response from individuals representing the UN, Red Cross and MSF was one of major interest.

International Relief Market Background
The need to respond rapidly and efficiently to natural disasters or complex emergencies from NGO's, government and relief agencies has never been greater. At this time, there are currently 22 million people around the world who qualify as 'displaced persons' and are under the direct care of the United Nations High Commissioner for Refugees.

The UNHCR has budgeted $115 million (USD) to manage the cost and complexity of logistics and supply chain management for all of the projects under their control, including the procurement of goods and services, for the year 1999. Well over 80% of this sections procurement is for shelter

Currently, the immediate response to an emergency includes the shipment and distribution of large sheets of plastic (with poles for construction) at a cost of $40 each, to be distributed to families and individuals for makeshift shelters. As the relief effort becomes more organized and actual needs are assessed, tents are supplied as quickly as possible for the displaced population. These, however, are considerably more expensive, starting at $100 each, but decreasing in cost as the quantity increases. This does provide the purchaser with some economies of scale benefit. Not included in this price is the logistical cost of supplying the refugees with shelters twice.

According to the UNHCR Supply and Transport section, eighty percent of their budget is used for procurement of shelter and domestic supplies, meaning that the UNHCR alone had spent $92 million in this sector in the year 2000.

Advantages of Basic Shelters
Basic Shelters are energy efficient, cost effective, and utilize combinations of natural structural materials and reinforced plastic film. Each fire-retardant shelter is designed to deploy quickly and easily to create a living space that is clean, dry and warm.

Basic Shelter Facts:
·Cost US $83.00 per tent with a volume of 10,000 tents
·250 tents can be shipped per 4 x 10 x 7 palette
·Easier to transport large numbers of the tents (approximately 1190 Basic Shelters per C-130 aircraft, vs. 350 of the competitor's tents)
·Logistically, it replaces two delivery cycles for relief agencies (plastic sheeting first, then tents)
·Manufactured of reusable materials, naturally sourced
·Fully fire retardant
·Lighter (30 lbs. vs. 85 lbs.) than competing products for the same volume
·Faster and easier to set up (portable by one person with an 8 minute set up vs. the 2 person portable, 45 minute setup of competitors)

The Manufacturing Technology
Speed, modularity and cost are the key competitive factors of the manufacturing technology.

The most critical production factor of Basic Shelter is the development of an efficient heat-sealing process to decrease the manufacturing time to 3 minutes per Basic Shelter. This technology is also the basis for additional profit as many other licensable products can be derived.

Basic Shelter installation >

∧ Basic Shelter installed

pp. 46-55 "Food and Shelter" Bakery Group and Jeff Ponitz, Published by 306090, Inc.

306090 03 09 02

WAVE GARDEN

306090 03 09 | 02

A power plant that harnesses the energy of ocean waves, YUSUKE OBUCHI's project is also a utopian ideal—or, more real than you think

by Yusuke Obuchi

Floating along the California coastline, the Wave Garden is a prototype for a dual-function power plant and public park, oscillating with the ocean waves and cycles of energy demand. On Monday through Friday, it generates energy; during the weekends, depending on the demand of electricity during the week, the Wave Garden transforms into a public garden—thus changing from a space of production to one of recreation and consumption.

The core aim of this project is to navigate energy as it is defined by two types of waves. The first type of wave exists in the cosmological realm, as a natural phenomenon—the ocean wave; the second is a socially constructed wave created by the demand for electricity as generated by people's use of everyday objects such as computers, television and domestic appliances. Like the ocean wave with its own type of internal logic, the structural patterning of the social wave with its ebbing and flowing from day to night is based on natural cycles. The Wave Garden is situated between these two waves, transforming the kinetic energy of the ocean waves into the commodified form of energy electricity. It investigates two types of energy which exist in both natural and social environments, and sees how these elements inform and form architecture.

Energy requires a form of mediation in order to transform it from one state of being to

Yusuke Obuchi is a partner of oko, a New York and Los Angeles architecture and creative design collaborative with Jason King and Martina Schafer. Current projects include a residence in Los Angeles and a marina and mixed-use project in the Caribbean.

From 1997–2000 Obuchi was a visiting assistant professor of architecture at the University of Kentucky. He received his Bachelor of Architecture from the Southern California Institute of Architecture and his Master of Architecture from Princeton University.

Wave Garden was first presented as a Master's thesis project at the School of Architecture at Princeton University under thesis advisor Jesse Reiser, and was the subject of a solo exhibition at the Storefront for Architecture in May and June 2002.

pp. 56–67 "Wave Garden" ©2002 Yusuke Obuchi, Hal Foster and Jesse Reiser, Published by 306090, Inc.

∧Wave Garden at Princeton University

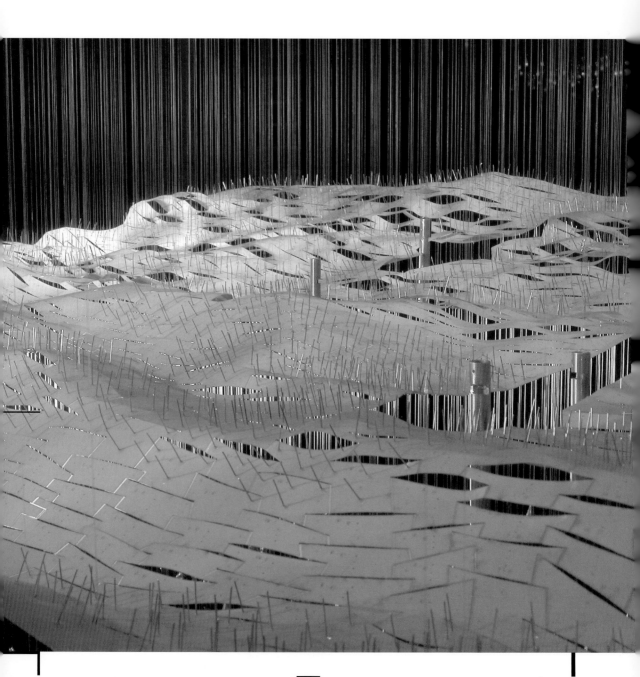

306090 03 09 02

another. Ocean waves are created by the wind, and differences in pressure and temperature in the surface of the Earth generate wind. In turn, differences in the atmosphere are caused by the rotational movement of the planet in relation to the position of the sun. Ocean water conducts energy moving continuously throughout the oceans on the earth; ocean waves are physical manifestations of energy. A wave is not an object moving across the water, rather it is the ocean transferring energy from one form to another. Ocean water is the medium in which wind transfers energy into wave.

The social demand for electricity behaves similarly to ocean waves. Like the energy that forms the wave, the flow of electricity emerges from a measurable demand produced by society, creating a rhythm that fluctuates according to natural temporal cycles such as the time of day, or the day of the week.

However, unlike energy occurring as a natural phenomenon, electric energy functions in society as a one-way system. It flows from a power plant through power lines, ending at an electric device. In order to achieve efficient energy production in the United States, the social demand and supply of electricity are carefully forecasted and energy is accordingly distributed through electrical infrastructure. In the case of California, the Independent System Operator (ISO), a central energy-controlling institution, oversees 80 percent of the state's energy demand, checking the consumption patterns every five minutes in order to forecast and direct the amount of energy production for individual power plants. The wave pattern of energy production reflects the degree of activities taking place in society.

The Wave Garden contains a built-in consumption control mechanism that acts as a 'reward system;' low energy consumption during the week is rewarded by a recreational space on the weekends. Reciprocally, the social wave of demand manipulates or changes the form and function of the Wave Garden. The demand or energy consumption statistics determine the shape and function of the Wave Garden during the weekend; it is a visual indicator, a physical record of California's energy consumption.

The area dedicated to recreation during the weekends is inversely proportional to the energy consumed during the week. If the weekly demand is low, the amount of space on the Wave Garden dedicated to recreational activity increases. If the weekly energy demand is too high, the garden is closed or the recreational area is reduced in size in order to dedicate more area for the production of energy to meet electrical needs. When the power plant lifts above the surface of the ocean, the

WORLD NET ELECTRICITY CONSUMPTION
1999   (Billion kilowatt / Hour)

United States	3,235.9
Japan	947.0
Canada	497.5
Germany	495.2
France	398.8
Mexico	170.9

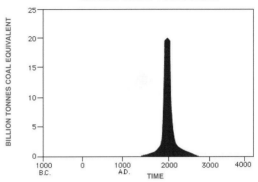

CONSUMPTION OF FOSSIL FUELS

COAL RESERVES   244 years left worldwide

Countries with the most coal reserves

*U.S. @ 270,901 million tons, or 23.7% of the world total
*Former U.S.S.R. @ 264,762 million tons, or 23.2% of the world total
*China @ 126,215 million tons, or 11.1% of the world total
*Australia @ 100,244 million tons, or 8.8% of the world total
*India @ 77,103 million tons, or 6.8% of the world total
*Germany @ 74,186 million tons, or 6.5% of the world total

Countries producing the most coal (per year)

*China @ 1,348 million tons, or 28.8% of the world total
*U.S. @ 988 million tons, or 21.1% of the world total
*India @ 333 million tons, or 7.1% of the world total
*Australia @ 265 million tons, or 5.7% of the world total
*Former U.S.S.R. @ 242 million tons, or 5.2% of the world total
*South Africa @ 220 million tons, or 4.7% of the world total
*Poland @ 201 million tons, or 4.3% of the world total

Countries consuming the most coal (per year)

*China @ 681.8 million tons oil equivalent, or 29.7% of the world total
*U.S. @ 527.9 million tons oil equivalent, or 23% of the world total
*India @ 146.4 million tons oil equivalent, or 6.4% of the world total
*Former U.S.S.R. @ 113 million tons oil equivalent, or 4.9% of the world total
*Japan @ 89.8 million tons oil equivalent, or 3.9% of the world total
*Germany @ 86.8 million tons oil equivalent, or 3.8% of the world total

PETROLEUM RESERVES   39 years left worldwide

Countries with the most petroleum reserves

*Saudi Arabia @ 261.5 billion barrels, or 25.2% of the world total
*Iraq @ 112.5 billion barrels, or 10.8% of the world total
*U.A.E. @ 97.8 billion barrels, or 9.4% of the world total
*Kuwait @ 96.5 billion barrels, or 9.3% of the world total
*Iran @ 93 billion barrels, or 9% of the world total
*Venezuela @ 71.7 billion barrels, or 6.9% of the world total
*Former U.S.S.R. @ 65.4 billion barrels, or 6.3% of the world total

pp. 56-67 "Wave Garden" ©2002 Yusuke Obuchi, Hal Foster and Jesse Reiser, Published by 306090, Inc.

Countries producing the most petroleum (per year)

*U.S. @ 9.35 million barrels/day, or 12.5% of the world total
*Saudi Arabia @ 8.46 million barrels/day, or 11.3% of the world total
*Former U.S.S.R. @ 7.22 million barrels/day, or 9.6% of the world total
*North Sea @ 6.15 million barrels/day, or 8.2% of the world total

Countries consuming the most petroleum (per year)

*U.S. @ 17.74 million barrels/day, or 24.8% of the world total
*Japan @ 5.79 million barrels/day, or 8.1% of the world total
*China @ 4.01 million barrels/day, or 5.6% of the world total
*Former U.S.S.R. @ 3.99 million barrels/day, or 5.6% of the world total

NATURAL GAS RESERVES 583 years left

Countries with the most natural gas reserves

*Former U.S.S.R. @ 1,700 trillion cubic ft, or 33.4% of the world total
*Iran @ 810 trillion cubic feet, or 15.9% of the world total
*Qatar @ 300 trillion cubic feet, or 5.9% of the world total
*U.A.E. @ 205 trillion cubic feet, or 4% of the world total
*Saudi Arabia @ 190 trillion cubic feet, or 3.7% of the world total

Countries producing the most natural gas (per year)

*U.S. @ 23,744 billion cubic feet, or 24.5% of the world total
*Former U.S.S.R. @ 21,005 billion cubic ft, or 21.7% of the world total

Countries consuming the most natural gas (per year)

*U.S. @ 622.8 cubic Gm, or 26.7% of the world total
*Former U.S.S.R. @ 371.1 cubic Gm, or 15.9% of the world total
*Germany @ 100.8 cubic Gm, or 4.3% of the world total

NUCLEAR RESERVES   42 years left worldwide

The quantity of nuclear reserves is as finite and limited as that of fossil fuels. Uranium Institute figures estimate the total world recoverable resources of uranium at 3,256,000 tons. Existing power plants operational worldwide require 75,000 tons of uranium a year to produce roughly 17% of the total world power requirements. The total resources will be sufficient to meet current and anticipated demand for only 42 years.

California 1999 Gross System Electricity Production

Resource Type	Gigawatt-Hours	Percentage
Hydro	41,617	15.09%
Nuclear	40,419	14.66%
Coal	36,327	13.17%
Oil	55	0.02%
Natural Gas	84,703	30.71%
Geothermal	13,251	4.80%
Biomass & Waste	5,663	2.05%
Wind	3,433	1.24%
Solar	838	0.30%
Imports - NW	26,051	9.45%
Imports - SW	23,436	8.50%
Total	275,793	100.00%

flexible surface transforms into a stable platform utilized as recreational space. Pulled down below the ocean, the Wave Garden becomes a shallow pool of water functioning as a beach.

The area of the Wave Garden measures 480 acres, approximately half the size of Central Park. Its surface consists of 1,734 tiled 3" thick piezoelectric membrane sheets and is supported by 1,734 tube buoys. Piezoelectric membrane is a flexible electric generator, which creates an electrical charge when bent or when stress is applied. The Wave Garden membrane consists of multiple positively and negatively charged layers, which become charged by the bending caused by the motion of the waves. Conversely, applying electric current to the membrane causes it to deform its physical shape. These two modes of material properties—one an electric generator, the other a form generator, define the physical condition of the Wave Garden.

The Wave Garden is accessible by boats departing from a terminal adjacent to the Diablo Canyon power plant. Every weekend, selected areas of the Wave Garden are suspended by the series of vertical buoy tube structures, acting as a ceiling under which boats approach the entrances. Boats dock by one of fourteen cylindrical elevator towers located in the space created between the ocean surface and the underside of the Wave Garden. Visitors gain access to the public garden by way of elevator, passing through the membrane, observing the thinness of the Wave Garden's ground plane.

The membrane is supported from below by a series of tube-like buoys that are systematically regulated by an attached electric pump. Depending on its function, as a power plant or public garden, seawater is pumped in and out of the tube. The amount of seawater and air inside of the tube determines the buoyancy and therefore the physical formation of the Wave Garden, defining and redefining its height in relation to sea level. Structures on land deal primarily with downward loads based on gravitational pull; this system utilizes both gravitational pull and the buoyancy of water as its structural system. The surface system of interlocking membrane panels form a pattern reflecting the contours of the ocean bed beneath. By mirroring that form, the Wave Garden functions in the most effective manner, flexing with the motion of the ocean waves.

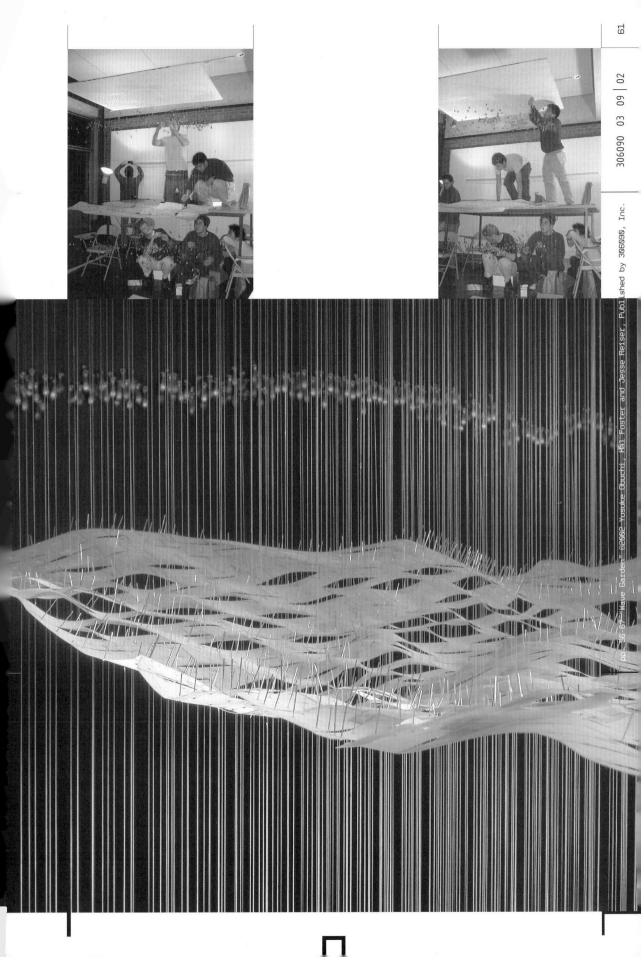

306090 03 09 | 02

pp. 56-67 "Wave Garden" ©2002 Yusuke Obuchi, Hal Foster and Jesse Reiser, Published by 306090, Inc.

Wave Garden at *ELECTRIC* Generator Mode - Weekdays Operation
(Wave motion bends Piezoelectric membrane, generating electricity)

1

Piezoelectric membrane

ELECTRIC GENERATOR

V_{out}
(Voltage output)

W (Size)

Piezoelectric membrane

F (Stretching input / Force)

2

Electricity produced

WAVE FORCE

ENERGY OUTPUT

$$V_{out} = g\,31\,\frac{F}{W}$$

Piezoelectric Voltage Constant
(Mechanical to electrical conversion)

Piezoelectrics: materials respond mainly to tension and compression
along their pulling **F** axis

3

WAVE FORCE

Electricity produced

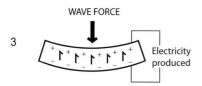

Wave Garden at *FORM* Generator Mode- Weekends Operation
(Electricity is appiled to Piezoelectric membrane, forming the Wave Garden)

1

+ + + + + +
– – – – – –

Piezoelectric membrane

FORM GENERATOR

V_{in}
(Voltage input)

W (Size)

Piezoelectric membrane

F (Stretching output / Deformation)

2

MEMBRANE DEFORMATION

Electricity applied

DEFORMATION OUTPUT

$$F_{out} = \frac{V_{in}\,W}{g\,31}$$

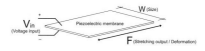

3

Electricity applied

MEMBRANE DEFORMATION

❯ Plan Diagram

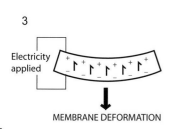

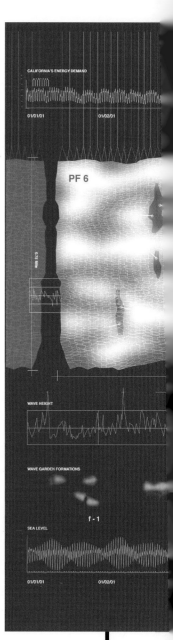

CALIFORNIA'S ENERGY DEMAND

01/01/01   01/02/01

PF 6

WAVE HEIGHT

WAVE GARDEN FORMATIONS

f - 1

SEA LEVEL

01/01/01   01/02/01

Anchored by way of a parachute anchor, the Wave Garden floats approximately one mile off shore from the nuclear power plant it will someday replace. Along the California coastline the Diablo Canyon nuclear power plant was the last nuclear power plant to be built in the United States (in 1986). The Wave Garden is a prototype designed to succeed the plant after its 40-year license expires in the year 2026.

306090 03 09 | 02

pp. 56-67 "Wave Garden" ©2002 Yusuke Obuchi, Hal Foster and Jesse Reiser, Published by 306090, Inc.

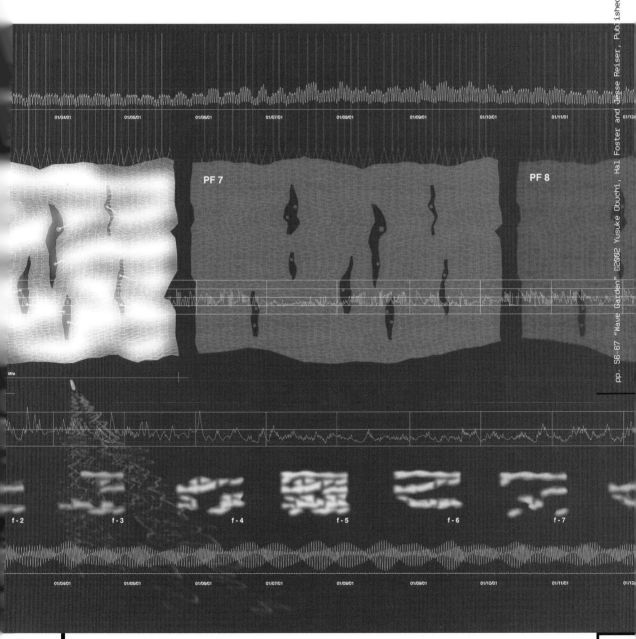

WAVE GARDEN
ARCHITECTURE IN A DYNAMIC MILIEU

by Jesse Reiser

It is perhaps no accident that Yusuke Obuchi, an itinerant expatriate since the age of sixteen, so clearly intuits the possibilities of change in a profession whose codes have traditionally valorized gravity, permanence and stasis.

His thesis, the Wave Garden project, which I had the privilege to advise, is exemplary of an emerging tendency in architecture that looks for new possibilities through the close tracking of material logics as they are released by dynamical systems. Simply put, he poses the question: what are the effects on our most commonly held architectural assumptions when its scales, orders and materials are traversed by energy fields?

His is a project that explores not fixed schemas but organizations that can become vehicle of continuous conversion, a material index of the First Law of Thermodynamics: that energy cannot be created or destroyed, it can only be converted into new forms. There is a rigor and an assumption within this direction of work and thought that the scales, systems and materials of architecture must be intimately linked so as to register and transmit the widest range of change at all levels.

These are poised and exquisitely sensitive systems—systems, moreover, that while intellectually and aesthetically engaging by themselves, present their most startling possibilities when properly aimed within the social and political context of building large-scale public works. Issues of nature and culture, of energy, work and excess—domains until recently considered in dialectical opposition to one another—have come to be seen within the elastic model of ecology and thus demand an architecture that will communicate within this larger constellation as well.

In a real sense, this project is a colossal mediator of environmental flows, delaying, transmitting and re-routing them for architecture on their way to entropy. This is an architecture of dissipative systems that cascade through scales, orders and materials, each with its own duration and effects. Such a deformation of ground never merely a formal salience but part of a continuum of flow; here converting an acre-sized parcel of artificial ground into a temporary hill of potential energy, there releasing potential through an energetic cascade into material scales.

Materials have also been re-evaluated, being chosen not solely for their traditional qualities but, as for example with the Piezoelectric membrane that can convert mechanical energy into electrical, become media of transfer. Here it is worth noting that the origins of these materials as a product of the war machine do not become problematic being from a critical stand point, which tends to judge and interpret them by virtue of their origins or history. Rather,

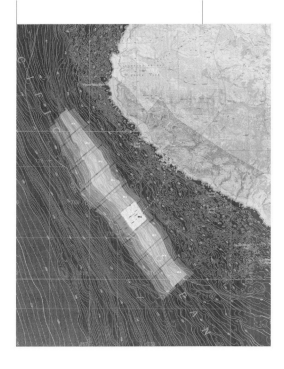 

306090 03 09 | 02

pp. 56-67 "Wave Garden" ©2002 Yusuke Obuchi, Hal Foster and Jesse Reiser, Published by 306090, Inc.

they are seen in their immediate capacity to produce effects and thus enter into the ethical domain of practice for what they can become rather than what they were.

Finally, I believe, it would be a mistake to consign this work to the melancholy history of utopian projects, or at least a utopian project that speaks to a yearning for a more perfect and purified future. The abstraction of the model speaks more to the mechanic aspects of the project—the lack of specificity to the constraints of time in school. Indeed this project would welcome contamination as the paradigms that underlie it are structured on difference rather than similarity.

This work above all is an experiment with the real, its engagement with abstract and material systems is not idealizing or autonomous—not a retreat from the world—but like any fine instrument, offers the most robust and open possibility to effect change within it.

"Architecture in a Dynamic Mileu", by Jesse Reiser, is printed here for the first time. Reiser is Professor of Architecture at the School of Architecture, Princeton University.

WAVE GARDEN
ATLANTIS FOUND IN THE PACIFIC

by Hal Foster

The Wave Garden by Yusuke Obuchi is a 480-acre rectangle that floats, like a Suprematist square, off the coast of California. Made up of 1,800 Piezoelectric sheets supported by 1,800 buoys, it serves as an electrical generator during the weekend and a marine park on the weekend. In its first mode the sheets of the garden are bent by the sea waves in a way that generates electricity that is then transferred to the energy grid of the Golden State. In its second mode electricity is run through the sheets in a way that shapes them into a metamorphic island of coastal leisure and maritime play.

When the project was first presented for review at Princeton, it was discussed as potentially functional, just crazy enough to work. That purchase on the possible is important to its effects, for otherwise the Wave Garden could be dismissed as another architectural whim. But the conversation got stuck in the viability of the project, which was also crazy (even if Sun Ra became President, the project could not be realized: no way in hell). In short, the Wave Garden is not whimsical, yet neither is it practical; it is precisely utopian, and it is this dimension that renders it both liberatory and critical, as is true of all utopian proposals. For it forces us, if only for a moment, to think "why not?," and the force of this why-not is to open up and to critique, if only for a moment, what-is.

The project will evoke different precedents for different viewers. In its presentation this floating garden looks more like a hanging garden, its sheets aglow and its wires and weights brilliant with reflected light. This apparition first reminded me of the structural demonstrations that Gaudi made for his La Familia Sagrada with its model vaults also hung with tiny weights to test how much load they might withstand. Like Gaudi Obuchi is both a rationalist and a visionary (they also share a fascination with tropes of wind and wave); both architects reconcile the Constructivist and the Surrealist lines in modernist form-making—Gaudi before this opposition quite existed; Obuchi in its apparent aftermath. (But are we ever done with these lines, or does the Constructivist-Surrealist dialectic only return in ever new guises?)

For most viewers the immediate parallels for the Wave Garden will be the Earthworks of the 1960s and 70s, but it sits uneasily in this genealogy. It might be reminiscent of another California dream, the Running Fence of Christo, but it is the Running Fence with brains that retain a social conscience. Richard Serra once remarked that Earthworks, like Running Fence, were just drawings at an environmental scale, but in a sense they are worse: they are expressionism (read narcissism) writ large as well. The Wave Garden is wondrously altruistic in comparison with such projects. It also does not partake of the fascination with entropy so evident in the

306090 03 09 | 02

Published by 306090, Inc.

©2002 Yusuke Obuchi, Hal Foster and Jesse Reiser,

pp. 56-67 "Wave Garden"

Earthworks of Robert Smithson, a reflection on the down side of the boom economy of the 1960s. On the contrary, the Wave Garden works to generate energy rather than to submit to its doom-day dissipation. And yet it is also not as redemptive as it may first appear. Early on Robert Morris was sensitive to the ideological recuperation of the Earthwork idea—that despoilers of the environment might use Earthworks as so much fill-in or camouflage. This is a danger that the Wave Garden also skirts: it is pragmatic, not pastoral. Unlike many designers in the present, Obuchi does not seek to naturalize—to vitalize or to animate—his architecture. On the contrary, his project is continuous with the greater human project to acculturate nature, but it proposes a taming, not a perverting. And in the end it might only point to the impossibility of such taming, to the utter wildness of the "Pacific" Ocean, to the sheer alterity of nature. For anyone who knows the sea at all knows that it would scatter this garden within a week, if not a day.

So what is the genre in play here? We might be tempted to say "science fiction," but such a reply might only admit our own distance from the utopian imagination. Grandiose projects call out for grandiose connections, so why not juxtapose the Wave Garden project with the Tatlin proposal for the Monument to the Third International (1919–20)? Projected to be far taller than the Eiffel Tower, the

Monument was to emblematize the new Communist society on the march. A spiral within a spiral, with struts made of steel, it was to house the various agencies of the government set in glass geometries, which were to rotate at various speeds (once a day, a week, a month, a year). A dialectical machine, it was also a figure of dialectics, one which was to harness the new forces of industrial technology in productive tension with the old rhythms of the natural world. Like the Wave Garden, the Monument could never be built, but its utopian quality guarantees its critical force to this day. A little of the same force might be put into play by the Wave Garden. Of course Tatlin had the State behind him, while Obuchi has only the Storefront. But even utopias start small.

Atlantis Found in the Pacific, by Hal Foster, is reprinted from "Wave Garden, Yusuke Obuchi," Storefront for Art and Architecture. Foster is Townsend Martin Professor of Art and Archaeology at Princeton University

A BRONX OLYMPICS

CCNY

Urban design students at City College envision a New York Olympics to rejuvenate the industrial Bronx waterfronts

306090 03 09 02

pp. 68-79 "A Bronx Olympics" ©2002 Michael Sorkin and CCNY, Published by 306090, Inc.

by Michael Sorkin

It's getting down to the wire on New York City's bid for the 2012 Olympics. In November, the U.S. Olympic committee will choose among competing proposals from New York, San Francisco, and Baltimore/Washington to host the games. Publicists and supporters are gung-ho, extravagant in their enthusiasm for the project, representing it to the public as an unvarnished good.

The New York City bid has been prepared by NYC 2012, a private nonprofit organization founded in 1998 by Daniel Doctoroff, presently the deputy mayor for economic development, who was, at that time, managing partner in Oak Hill Capital Partners, an investment firm established with Robert Bass. The physical plan has been executed under the direction of Alex Garvin, a City Planning Commissioner and currently planning director of the Lower Manhattan Development Corporation. The key roles played by Doctoroff and Garvin (as well as the support of the Mayor and the local government) surely give the plan a sense of official imprimatur.

But why should a city host the Olympics in the first place? Why expend the time, cash, and energy to attract an event that lasts only three weeks? And why—given the very mixed financial, social, environmental, and ethical results of other recent games—should the public have positive expectations for the Olympics? Despite NYC 2012's claim that two out

Michael Sorkin is an architect and writer based in New York. He is the director of the Graduate Urban Design program at the City College of New York.

Students:

Orit Norman-Dor
Gustavo Gonzalez
Silvia Jenatschke
Burak Kasopoglu
Jair Laiter

All images courtesy of CCNY

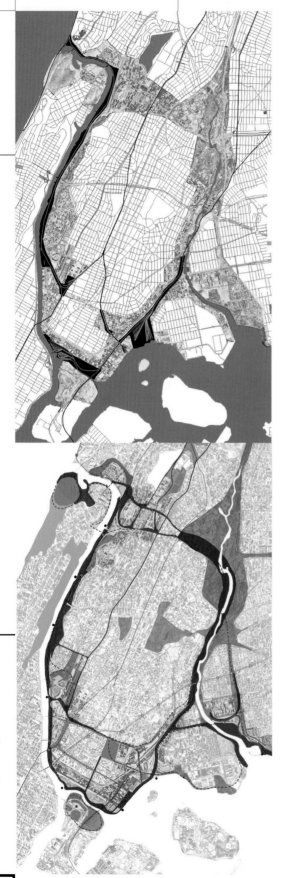

306090   03   09 | 02

of three New Yorkers "support" the games, basic questions must still be asked about both their logic in general and this plan in particular.

Olympic advocates generally suggest two reasons for hosting the games—prestige and money. The argument for prestige is most persuasively offered by second-tier cities—like Salt Lake City or Atlanta—that aspire to "world class" status, to put themselves on the map. While that's not exactly NYC 2012 nevertheless argues that the Olympics will provide "a celebration of community spirit," presumably boosting the "if you can make it there, you can make it anywhere" ethos that New Yorkers cleave to axiomatically. From the standpoint of pure prestige, the issue is a wash.

The issue of money raises a more important set of questions, most significantly, where it is to come from and who will get it. Olympic funding is generated from two sources: income and subsidy. On the income side, the three main streams are broadcast rights, ticket sales, and licensing deals, from corporate sponsorships to the manufacture of souvenirs. NYC 2012 projects revenues of $3.3 billion from the games (a reasonable sum, given that the 2000 Olympics in Sydney earned $1.3 billion alone), against operating expenses of $2 billion, and construction costs of $1.3 billion.

When compared to the plans proposed, however, these numbers immediately beg the question of subsidy. Ever since the Los Angeles games of 1984—organized by a private business coalition, housed largely in existing facilities, and generating an operating surplus of $225 million—the model for the games has been entrepreneurial. Given the telling and widespread critique that the games disproportionately benefit business interests at the expense of public programs for the poor, no Olympic proposal can be sold without the claim that it will produce some positive, general economic benefit. It would need to promise that it will not require public funds. In fact, recent Olympics have involved ever increasing amounts of subsidy. The federal contribution has, for example, risen from $75 million for Los Angeles to $608 million for Atlanta to a staggering $1.3 billion for Salt Lake City.

The NYC 2012 proposal is very much in the post–Los Angeles Olympics format. The plan makes efficient use of existing facilities—astutely distributed among the boroughs and New Jersey—but proposes to build a number of others, most notably a large "Olympic Stadium" over the West Side rail yards and an Olympic Village at Queens West. The overall scheme is organized along two long circulation axes that form an "X"— one branch on the water extending down the Harlem and East Rivers and across the harbor to Staten Island, the other a rail axis

along existing lines that runs from Flushing Meadows through midtown and out to Giants Stadium. Thus dispersed, the plan offers a little something for everyone.

There are two exceptions to this disaggregated approach, both advertised as major public benefits. The first is the proposed Olympic Village in Queens West—at the crossing of the "X"—which organizers contend will offer 4,400 units of "affordable" housing after the games. But this is a development that is already in the works, and a 2012 date is unlikely to accelerate its completion. Nor is there any guarantee of the "affordability" of the project, should it be undertaken under Olympic auspices.

The second major "from scratch" element in the scheme is the construction of the main Olympic stadium over the rail yards next to the Javits Center. This proposal grows out of long-standing plans to expand Javits and to build a football stadium for the émigré Jets, a scheme particularly beloved by politicians but of dubious logic with regard to other potential uses for the site and a potential traffic nightmare. And, of course, public financing for major league stadiums is immediately suspicious, and such situations have a history of turning out to be a swindle. Although the details are murky, it seems likely that this stadium will soak up the major portion of the Olympic construction account. However, its viability—given the site's distance from public transportation—is predicated on the investment of billions to extend the number seven subway from Times Square to the stadium, as well as on a raft of other infrastructure improvements in the neighborhood. Although NYC 2012 claims that "no tax dollars would be used to conduct the games," it is clear that without many tax dollars, the games cannot be conducted.

The construction of the stadium also fits into larger plans by the current administration to focus development energy on midtown south. Indeed, one of the first projects initiated by Doctoroff as deputy mayor was a large-scale planning study of the area, which presupposed the construction of a stadium.

The NYC 2012 proposal argues that were the Olympics to happen here, "the New York/New Jersey region could expect tens of thousands of new jobs and a local economic impact approaching $11 billion." This impressive sum may well be on the money. It is undeniable that hosting the Olympics creates jobs, but, considering the short-term, low-wage type of employment that tends to be generated (witness Atlanta) and the potential downsides of the Olympics, the real question—unanswered—is whether it's worth it, given the range of possible investments.

pp. 68–79 "A Bronx Olympics" ©2002 Michael Sorkin and CCNY, Published by 306090, Inc.

✓ Transportation strategy

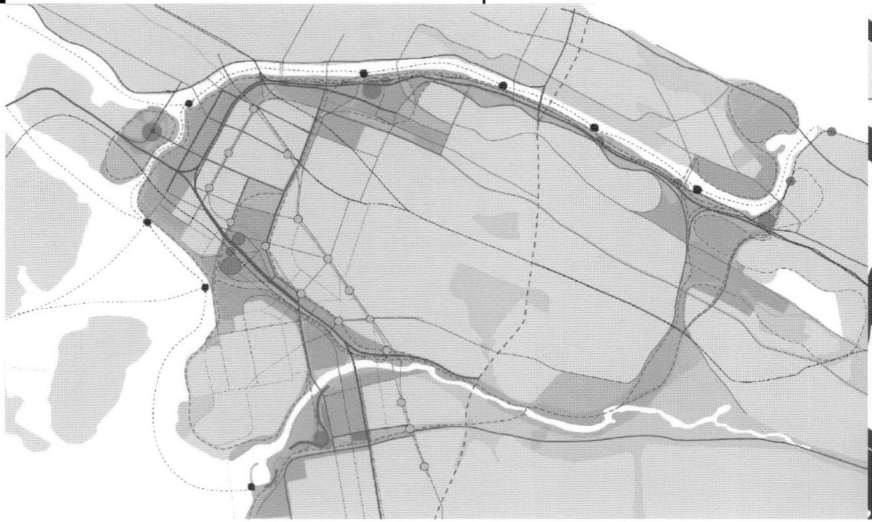

✓ Industrial sites

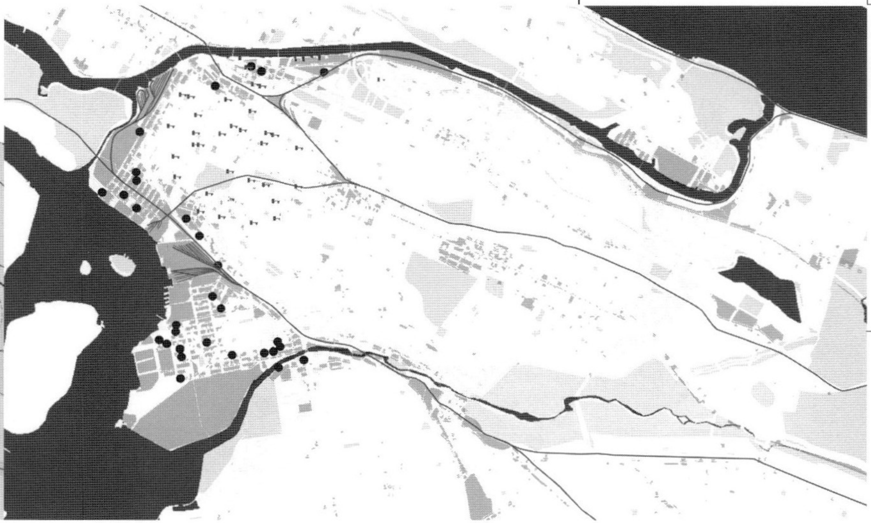

306090 03 09 | 02

NYC 2012 claims that its plan will act as "a catalyst for improving housing, parks, and transportation, and other key pieces of the city's infrastructure to form a lasting legacy for the city's growth." Here we reach the nub of the appeal of the Olympics, the idea that it has a social and economic value beyond the short-term benefit of a hyperspectacular tourism engine. The model here is Barcelona, a city that aggressively used its Olympics to transform the city. Although it has been argued that this transformation was purchased at the expense of the poor, the visible legacy of that Olympics is decidedly impressive as is the boost given to the city's international aura. The question for New York is whether such good physical outcomes can be purchased in such a way that those most in need will be the primary beneficiaries, not commercial interests.

This possibility for real synergy was the speculation that motivated the research of the CCNY graduate urban design studio in spring 2001. We set out to examine an alternative scheme for a New York City Olympics, one in which the games were concentrated in a single area of the city with particularly dire physical and economic needs. The scheme proposed by NYC 2012, although ingenious in its organization, is unlikely to have much lasting benefit for New York City neighborhoods. Is there another way? What might be the outcome of an Olympic games dedicated not to advancing the interests of the real estate industry in the development of southwest midtown, but to jolting moribund and disinvested neighborhoods back to life—a genuinely popular Olympics?

The scheme developed by the students at CCNY locates Olympic activity in a continuous swath along the Harlem and East River waterfront of the Bronx. It makes extensive use of existing facilities and benefits from the existing saturation of the area by rail lines, roadways, and other means of transport. It would also redress the dereliction and disuse along the Bronx waterfront, now suffering long post-industrial neglect but potentially a ravishing area. To be sure, the project is visionary, neither the product of long consultation nor necessarily the only large-scale strategy for the revitalization of the waterfront. But it is a strategy focused on the long term and on people, not profit.

The CCNY plan is based on a series of principles which might be generally applied to urban Olympics projects but which have special resonance in the South Bronx, historically one of the city's most bereft locale.

1 — Invest in Areas that Need Investment

This would seem to be a slam-dunk for the Bronx. The urgency of riverfront renovation, toxic clean-up, housing construction, and job creation is nowhere greater in New York City. Using the Olympics to vitalize struggling neighborhoods and businesses would give the games both a focus and a purpose. The Bronx sites thus have the advantage both of immediate adjacency to neighborhoods in need of a boost and of the availability near those neighborhoods of major, unencumbered sites with excellent accessibility.

2 — Reinforce Existing Neighborhoods and Centers

A successful Olympic intervention will do more for the Bronx than simply lie in a fine armature for sports. Careful placement of facilities can both generate economic activity and stitch together places rent in twain. For example, this scheme proposes to build its Olympic Village over the rail-yards at the southern tip of the Bronx in order to provide housing (with spectacular southern exposures and views) and to link the Bronx with Randall's Island and Manhattan. A group of smaller facilities, which sit on a structure above the rail lines that divide the area of the Grand Concourse from the Bronx Hub, could promote an elision that will join a series of existing institutions (including nearby Hostos College), neighborhoods, and commercial centers.

3 — Make Permanent Improvements in Transportation and Infrastructure

This plan also proposes to build the Olympic/Football Stadium in the industrial area of Port Morris, adjacent to the Bruckner Expressway, near several subways, and over the main northbound Amtrak/Metro-North rail line. By including a large amount of parking, this site would accommodate stadium crowds for football and other post-Olympic events and would provide a park and ride facility for commuters from the northern suburbs who might switch to Metro-North or Amtrak from the subway, express busses, or ferries. The plan also proposes three additional Metro-North stations (in easily built, on-grade locations), a series of ferry stops, and additional parking accessible directly from existing express-ways, keeping traffic off local streets.

4 — Use the Olympics to Leverage Borough-Wide Improvements

One of the scheme's major proposals is to create a "Bronx Ring," a continuous green space girdling the borough. Building upon ongoing efforts to renaturalize the Harlem and Bronx rivers, this ring would provide continuous space-linking, for example, the

pp. 68–79 "A Bronx Olympics" ©2002 Michael Sorkin and CCNY, Published by 306090, Inc.

New York Botanical Gardens

BRO...

PARK

New York Zoological Gardens

Fort Tryon Park

Claremont Park

CROTONA PARK

Hunt's Point Market

RANDALL'S ISLAND PARK

Rikers Island

306090 03 09 | 02

Bronx Zoo and the Botanical Garden-for pedestrians, bikers, and other species. Most importantly, it would be a highly image-able shared space uniting the communities of the south Bronx. Ultimately, it could be the foundation for a green network in northern New York City that might sprout as tendrils from the Ring.

5 — Pursue a Mixed Use Strategy

There is no reason why a sports stadium should remain merely a sports stadium. Particularly in the case of facilities that are in use only a small portion of the time, the imperative is to find ways to provide continuous regular animation and economic activity for neighborhoods. Stadiums should be generators, not simply consumers: housing, schools, public facilities, office and industrial space could be part not only of the stadium complex, but part of the stadium itself.

Moreover, one of the benefits of placing large-scale stadiums in industrial areas is that they are themselves organized industrially-they are huge machines that move very large numbers of people in and out over a relatively short period of time. Such attributes are not compatible-unless carefully modulated-with the intimate rhythms of traditional neighborhoods.

6 — Be Clear On Post-Olympic Outcomes.

The reason to have an Olympics in New York City, given the expense, disruption, and effort involved must be some large and lasting benefit to the city as a whole. Certainly the construction and renovation of athletic and recreational facilities can be useful (if done in such a way to benefit maximum participants and not merely professional teams) and the infusion of tourist dollars can offer a major, if transient, economic boost. But an expenditure of this magnitude should be ambitious, should provide the city with permanent benefits at a scale that will be both legible and very helpful to those who need help most.

Why not a Bronx Olympics?

pp. 68-79 "A Bronx Olympics" ©2002 Michael Sorkin and CCNY, Published by 306090, Inc.

Hybrid Waterfront, Longwood

The Program for a Bronx Olympics demands the construction of several stadiums, the most central of which is the Olympic stadium. This 100,000 spectator stadium is proposed to remain as home to the Giants after the 2012 Olympiad. After thorough analysis, we found a potential site for an object of such scale in a lost land that lays to the south of the Major Deegan Expressway in the southernmost tip of the Bronx. The site is an abandoned and derelict area touching and bordering a few different neighborhoods such as Mott Haven and Port Morris. Other areas include the industrial quarter of Longwood and the underused freight Amtrak train tracks. This unclaimed post industrial wasteland sits today on prime waterside properties with metropolitan views. The abandonment of such neighborhoods can be attributed to many forces, from transportation mistakes to policies in housing.

This project aims to identify the physical relationships resulting from uncontrolled growth of urban pockets of different uses (industrial, residential, commercial, and civic) on the south Bronx. The most prevalent presence in the site is that of infrastructure, the highway, the industrial artifacts and their contrast between scales- of metropolitan and regional transit, and of citywide industrial lands. An evident disparity between them brings questions of compatibility, both in terms of program and use, and in terms of form and character. How can we reconcile a power plant or a steel factory with a public school and a landmark row house neighborhood? How well do such contrasting conditions invite the addition of an Olympic stadium or villa? These became the driving questions for this project.

This zoning conflict, overwhelming and untamable at first sight, became promising as it held huge potential for a flexible and audacious approach. The main objective of this project explored and exploited the potential of generating unexpected relationships between typically unconciliable land uses. This project seeks to devise as many synergies as possible between the site's autonomous components and a diverse use of new program. It is driven by contrasts, friction, contradiction, simultaneity, and aims to find solutions to apparently unsolvable problems of adjacency. Typical modes of urban planning and design find immediate hesitation in such combinations, but why? The incorporation and integration of different uses, programs, typologies became the challenge to overcome in this project. The very space of friction between these apparently unrelated objects here becomes a site of fertility to grow a truly mixed use cityscape in this wasted waterfront of New York City. JAIR LAITER

Jair Laiter was born in Mexico City. He has studied Art History at the Universidad Ibero-Americana, architecture at Pratt and the California College of Arts and Crafts where he received a Bachelor of Architecture and has worked as an architect in Mexico Japan, and the US. He received a Master in Urban Design at CCNY in 2001 and currently works at Michael Sorkin Studio.

Longwood site plan

North Bronx Neighborhoods

Program:
    Basketball Stadium
    Cycling Track
    Field Hockey Stadium
    Mountain Biking Track

This project creates a new set of relationships between neighborhoods through different layers of activities, creating new meeting points and pedestrian paths, and connecting divided space. Taking advantage of the riverfront site's complex section, one of the new stadiums will be built into the cross-section of the elevated train platform to generate a gathering place for different groups, at the same time, changing the visual characteristics of the skyline along the river edge.

Considering many levels spatially, culturally and functionally, the idea of offering an exchange point that will bring to the Bronx/Upper Manhattan area prosperity becomes a major issue. Connections can be seen as the solution to the social conflicts, both locally and within the Olympic international community. The layering of public spaces and meeting points where only the individual building makes the difference—articulated as a system—may be interpreted as seed for social reproductions requiring and producing cultural actions.   GUSTAVO GONZALEZ

Gustavo A. Gonzalez was born in Neiva, Colombia. He received his undergraduate degree in architecture from Los Andes University, Bogotá and his Masters in Urban Design from City College of New York. He has worked for the Michael Sorkin Studio, Rogers Marvel Architects, C.C.A.C. architectural office, Ahari & Associates Architects, all in New York City.

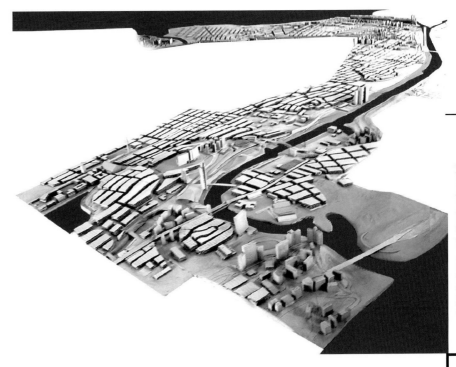

pp. 68-79 "A Bronx Olympics" ©2002 Michael Sorkin and CCNY, Published by 306090, Inc.

⟨ North Bronx neighborhoods model
North Bronx neighborhoods plan ⟩

Yankee Stadium—Mount Eden Site

Program:
    Soccer stadium and training arena
    Stadium for handball and badminton
    Stadium for volleyball and table tennis
    Stadium for rhythmic gymnastics

This scheme activates the three major unused spaces on the site–space beneath the expressway, air rights above railway easements, and abandoned building plots–to stitch together a new Olympic Village on the fringes of a Bronx neighborhood. The large concentration of empty building lots make for convenient new stadium sites. By burying the railways and decking over the yards to create a public plaza above, a new connection is made between the Olympic site south along the riverfront and the existing Yankee Stadium. The utilization of these new connections also provides for an enhanced relationship between the newly created waterfront green spaces.

Silvia Jenatschke holds a diploma in architectural engineering from the University Friderican in Karlsruche, Germany and has worked for several firms in both Karlsruche and New York. She is currently enrolled in the urban design program at CCNY.

SYLVIA JENATSCHKE

> Mount Eden site model

South Bronx Olympic Park with Olympic Village

Olympic Program:
  Beach volleyball
  Diving and Swimming Facilities
  Stadium for Fencing/ Judo/ Table Tennis/ Taekwondo/ Weight lifting/ Wrestling
  Tennis Facilities
  Olympic Village—accommodation for 15,000   athletes, trainers and officials plus parking Commercial and Public Facilities
  Event Parking

This project, in addition to creating a new skyline for the Bronx, provides the required amount of programmatic space for the Olympics, while connecting the neighborhood with the waterfront and Randall's Island. The siting also provides easy access for pedestrians and cyclists. The facilities are intended to remain after the events conclude. The new village and recreational facilities will provide much needed revenue for the Bronx in the future as well, with the addition of housing and commercial areas along Bruckner Boulevard. Railways will provide transportation for goods into the area to reduce vehicular traffic. Truck access is provided via the Triboro Bridge directly into a lower level receiving area. The rail yard is also integrated into the Triboro Bridge entrance. The space above is converted into greenways—designed as an elevated park and houses the Olympic stadiums. Two pedestrian and one cyclist bridge will connect Randall's Island with the site, connecting the Tennis facilities to this newly revitalized area. A new bus terminal is located parallel to the bridge as well. A new subway station connects the center of the village with the proposed Second Avenue subway system. A greenway is provided by burying the Major Deegan Expressway, also creating a buffer zone to the noise from pollution and noise.

ORIT NORMAN-DOR

Orit Norman-Dor was born if Haifa Israel and holds a bachelors degree from the Sadna College of Architecture and Design in Tel Aviv as well as a bachelor of architecture from Pratt. She received her Masters in Urban Design from CCNY in 2001 and is currently working in New York.

306090 03 09 | 02

pp. 68-79 "A Bronx Olympics" ©2002 Michael Sorkin and CCNY, Published by 306090, Inc.

South Bronx site model
South Bronx site plan

THREE PROJECTS

Archeworks

The responsibility of living within a modern society requires its citizens to learn to reside and communicate with each other. Often, we have failed in altruism. But, in an optimistic way, we have also triumphed time and again in coming together to aid those in dilemma. It is in this spirit that Archeworks engages its context.

There are numerous issues throughout the world that need solutions, which cannot be resolved in a simple manner. In 1994, the co-founders of Archeworks, Eva Maddox and Stanley Tigerman, situated their school in Chicago—a city with a "hands-on" tradition. Archeworks hopes that by acting locally, an application can be found globally. The heart of their work is an intent to integrate design holistically and ethically, in order to aid those who need it most.

Some citizens lack appropriate physical environments. Many live in crime-ridden communities battling for basic necessities like health care, education, and child care assistance. Instead of resolving the problem at hand, many politicians delegate surface resolutions that only grant money—but do not solve ongoing problems.

The programmatic aim at Archeworks is to expose students to the problems not typically covered in established educational institutions. The mission of Archeworks is to address social needs by developing and providing alternative design and education solutions through a multi-disciplinary process.

Because most difficulties of common life are wrapped in the intricacies of modus operandi, Archeworks counteracts this by drawing from a multiplicity of people with diverse disciplines and backgrounds—such as architecture, interior design, industrial design, art, engineering, law, creative writing, film, medicine, graphic design and sociology—who are led by facilitators that offer alternatives to mainstream thinking. Looking at the problems of today on a multi-disciplinary team, Archeworks students have the chance to reconfigure, respond and design the essential contemporary needs in a socially conscious way. Insight is gained through working closely with "focus groups" consisting of end-users as well as seasoned professionals. Through this collaboration Archeworks succeeds in fostering alternative careers and provides choices in the discipline that are socially responsible. Students deepen their understanding of successful application for theory and practice in nontraditional contexts where historical patterns and solutions do not apply.

Archeworks hopes that interdisciplinary approaches will become increasingly important to a society that is sorely in need of workable solutions to its most challenging issues.

306090 03 09 | 02

pp. 80-89 "Three Projects" ©2002 Archeworks, Published by 306090, Inc.

13 STAIRS

Santino Medina received a Bachelor of Science in Architecture from the University of Texas and a Certificate of Completion from Archeworks. He is currently compiling a book on the last eight years of Archeworks student projects.

Students:
Luc Gehant, Gunda Maurer, Santino Medina,
Jennifer Schaap, Kimberly Thomas

Facilitators:
Charles Smith and Anna Kania

Budget: $2,000

www.viewfromtheground.com

JUVENILE DETENTION

Anahita Anandam received a Master of Architecture from the College of Architecture + Urban Planning at the University of Michigan and a Bachelor of Architecture from Anna University, Madras, India. She holds a Certificate of Completion from Archeworks and currently works at OWP/P Architects in Chicago.

Students:
Anahita Anandam, Yasha Morehouse Amber, Owen Gerst,
Rosma Gutierrez, Donna Piacenza, Joshua Roberts

Facilitators:
Denise Arnold, Gerardo Fitz-Gibbons and Ammar Eloueini

Budget: $2,000

www.archeworks.org/work

DESIGN IN THE SOCIAL AGENDA

Sevra Davis received her undergraduate degree in architecture from Yale University and her Certificate of Completion from Archeworks. She has worked for Tigerman McCurry Architects in Chicago and is currently enrolled in the International Architecture program at the Helsinki University of Technology.

Students:
Jennifer Baker, Mary Davis, Sevra Davis,
David Harrell, Christina Hoxie, Lyn Payton

Facilitators:
Stanley Tigerman, Ben Nicholoson,
Douglas Garofalo, Michael Newman

Budget: $2,000

www.caseforgooddesign.org

THREE PROJECTS

13 STAIRS

by Santino Medina

Stateway Gardens, once the best hope for a public-housing development in Chicago, is now scheduled for demolition over a four- to five-year period. In its place, public-housing units in low-rise integrated structures are slated for construction—to be sold at market price. Archeworks is working with Stateway Gardens and the Department of Housing and Urban Development to identify which environmental elements are critical to residents undergoing transition. Archeworks role is to identify a vocabulary of transition, wherein certain cultural elements or aspects of family histories specifically associated with the existing surroundings may be preserved during and after construction. Through this collaboration, the team actively integrated current public housing residents with their new, more affluent neighbors.

An integral part of this research involved site visits. At Stateway Gardens, students toured the buildings with volunteers who walk the seventeen-story buildings on a daily basis—taking the stairs, the elevators rarely work—recording trash in the hallways, broken lights, vacant units and other discrepancies. This record is turned over to the Chicago Housing Authority (CHA), whose job—which rarely ever occurs—is to rectify these problems. The volunteers help residents with social and medical services and also in acquiring jobs. During the visits, students spoke with and interviewed residents about their circumstances, documenting their responses in writing and took photographs. Their introduction to a community that is rarely penetrated by outsiders—and which retains some insularity—revealed the loving and nourishing families that live off the dark corridors, where drug-dealing, gang-banging and substance addiction are common. Lifetime residents have adapted to the circumstances very well. The residents know that in the murky stairwells—where it can be pitch-black at midday—a person takes thirteen steps to get to the next floor. On the exceptional occasion an elevator is functional, one must punch a secret series of buttons to get to the desired floor.

An art program was started with a group of third graders at the local elementary school, where the students helped with local improvements, as well as with a variety of crafts. This was geared as a way in to the new community. These third graders would someday be the adults of the community. Many, who live without the "material necessities" of modern America, revel in their environment. If there were no tools available for an organized sport, they would invent a game—one time, dragging a mattress from a dumpster to use as a trampoline.

The managers who maintain these properties also had opinions to project. They face difficulties with both the city and with residents. Because of tight budgets, many building managers balance mainte-

306090 03 09 | 02

nance issues—including such basic needs as elevators, trash chutes and stairwell lighting.

Public housing architects also agree that there is indeed a dilemma to designing units that simultaneously fall under city regulations and meet the minimum standards of a home.

Recommendations for Stateway Gardens

Public awareness
A public awareness campaign could effectively demonstrate the plight of housing residents to the city of Chicago and the rest of the nation. At the same time it would address the community, informing residents of the city's plans for improvement. One design solution suggested that images and messages be projected on one of the seventeen story units, visible from the highway, commuter trains, and public transportation. Although this idea would be phenomenal if executed, the actual costs would be impractical, considering how many basic needs also lacked money.

Services
The neighborhood of Stateway Gardens currently lacks many services, like medical and social centers, groceries, museums and post offices. It would be useful to provide families in transition with a care package including a map during the transition period. Archeworks created a prototype map by studying 100 families, where they had moved and where the services available to them were located.

Spaces Surrounding Stateway Gardens
Stateway Gardens consists of thirty-three acres of land. Once occupied with six seventeen-story units and two ten-story units, it is now home to only four units. We felt we ameliorate the derelict and deserted condition by making improvements inside as well as outside, such as planting gardens, installing cooking grills, building play lots, creating gathering places, and installing simple items like benches— none of which currently exist. These things were all part of the once-thriving community of. Now— because of bureaucracy, the CHA—many of these ideas could not be executed or restored.

Plan B
In the event that for one reason or another CHA cancelled the plans for Stateway or money from private developers was "exhausted," we planned on going ahead with our improvements under the radar of CHA and local government.

Spring Event
The project began in September, but soon winter arrived and enveloped Stateway Gardens in a stratum of snow, devouring the buildings with cranes and bulldozers. Archeworks planned to hold an event for the Stateway community in the spring, demonstrating that this forsaken place contains great vitality. As existing public spaces are viewed negatively—as hotbeds of crime—this event would establish a new gathering center for residents of the community to trade information, while also providing a place to simply sit and enjoy the day. Due to weather conditions, this event has not taken place yet, but plans are still under way.

Results
Archeworks attempts to infringe upon mainstream institutions and impose an alternate view of how things could work. At times failing and at times succeeding— at times it has been hard to distinguish. Archeworks does not always attain a "product." Many times the product is the experience and the creation of ideas.

This project allowed all involved to meet a beautiful community steeped in history, family and friends that will affect all team members for a lifetime. In the process speaking with many who disagreed with the project, we made friends with people we might never have come into contact with; were challenged by a bureaucratic process; and, hopefully, were able to make small changes that have positively affected the world.

pp. 80-89 "Three Projects" ©2002 Archeworks, Published by 306090, Inc.

THREE PROJECTS

JUVENILE DETENTION

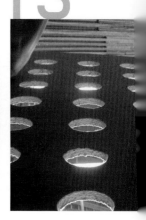

By Anahita Anandam

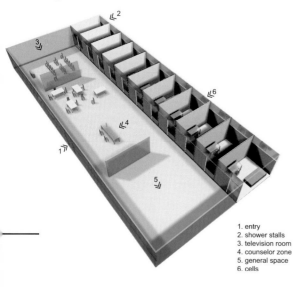

1. entry
2. shower stalls
3. television room
4. counselor zone
5. general space
6. cells

In an attempt to investigate the possibilities for improving overall design quality of criminal justice facilities, Archeworks students developed a model for a prototype detention center. The project focused on the design of a juvenile detention center that would, appropriately, support the juvenile rehabilitation process. With the help and cooperation of the Cook County Juvenile Detention Center—which works with children considered to be at "high risk" for future detention—post-detainees, judges, and community leaders, we were able to install a prototype model for a cell, called "the pod."

The research included a series of focus-group meetings conducted to comprehend not only the problems faced by juveniles in general, but those specific to the focus area, Chicago's South Lawndale neighborhood. The following facts about the Juvenile Justice System and social and spatial conditions within the Cook County Juvenile Detention Center were found particularly salient:

Cost of detaining juveniles is 6 times the cost of educating them
Rehabilitation programs are sparse
Juvenile detainees live in poor conditions
Outdoor activities are limited
Juveniles are often rejected by their former schools upon leaving the center
Job opportunities for former detainees are significantly lacking
Juvenile return rate is 60 percent

A lack of true rehabilitation and post-detention support at a juvenile detention center encourages youths into a cycle of detention and release, with few opportunities to return to be truly rehabilitated. This proposal attempts to break the existing cycle by providing opportunities for the rehabilitation of juvenile detainees and post-detainees.

The rehabilitation process is aided by providing the juveniles with a designed physical environment. This alternative design proposal rethinks the cell, transforming it into a fully customized pod within an existing cellblock, while simultaneously trying to reinforce

306090 03 09 | 02

80-89 "Three Projects" ©2002 Archeworks, Published by 306090, Inc.

a sense of communal co-existence. Using a system of points (which may be earned through improved behavior), a detainee would be able to transform a singular living space to a more shared one. The pods can be rearranged to form units of two, three, or four, sharing a common space.

The furniture within the pod can also be acquired as the juvenile progresses through different levels of rehabilitation. The furniture is modular and can easily plug in or be removed. As the juvenile detainees progress through the program, they earn plug-ins—clocks, shelves, drawing boards—for a pegboard that is built into the pod. The pod thus shapes itself to the needs of the inhabitant within it, as well as being influenced by the layout of the other pods in proximity. Sharing space within a community of peers becomes part of the experience.

Archeworks also proposes a mentorship program. As juveniles progress through the system, they take on the role of a mentor for incoming detainees. When the juvenile is released, the existing school program at the center would accept post-detainees, in order to maintain the relationship the juvenile might have built up with the mentor during their stay.

To effect change in a system that has been in place for many years now, one must employ slow, but distinct steps to implement new ideas. The first step was to introduce the pod concept into the existing Cook Country Juvenile Detention Center. The intent is to use the pod as a catalyst for change, ultimately encouraging awareness among leaders and members of the community in an effort rethink, transform, or even completely eliminate the existing model of a juvenile detention center.

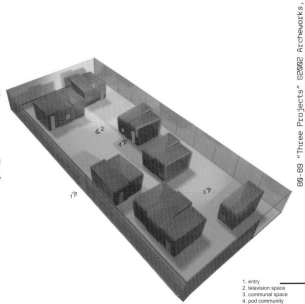

1. entry
2. television space
3. communal space
4. pod community

Proposed cell layout ›

THREE PROJECTS

DESIGN IN THE SOCIAL AGENDA

by Sevra Davis

This project was conceived and built on the premise that good design is generally withheld from those in most need of it. Observations over the past seven years at Archeworks have made it clear that design is not an area of focus or concern in areas of social need like public housing, penal systems, health care facilities, and eldercare centers. This project is built on the idea that good design enhances everyday life, serves the cohesion of a community, and works to preserve the environment; that is, good design serves a common good. Through collaboration with local architects, designers, and social activists, the team set out to research ways in which design is withheld from certain segments of society, thus determining how design may penetrate those same areas to provide for the common good.

The project began by drafting the following mission statement:

> We will investigate how to democratize good design with the ultimate goal of educating and promoting and awareness of the value of universal good design.

Our first challenge, then, was to define what is meant by the terms "design" and "good design."

306090 03 09 | 02

pp. 80-89 "Three Projects" ©2002 Archeworks, Published by 306090, Inc.

Next, the team wrote authored a manifesto in efforts to state opinions concerning the lack of good design in areas of social need. In the genre of the Futurist manifestoes of the early twentieth century, the resulting "The Case for Good Design" manifesto is a testament to the fervent opinions and emotions that are tied to this issue.

The research project culminated in a symposium titled "Making the Case: Good Design in the Social Agenda." The symposium—consisting of a series of panels, roundtable discussions and lectures, all free and open to the public—brought together theorists and practitioners in the fields of design and social activism to discuss the issue of design and social need. Another topic questioned whether our current state of capitalism and consumerism can effectively coexist with ethical and socially responsible design. The panelists, lecturers, and discussion leaders included: Denise Arnold, Sheila de Bretteville, Clive Dilnot, Bettina Drew, Jeanne Gang, Douglas Garofalo, Brad Lynch, Ben Nicholson, Jason Pickleman, Kent Spreckelmeyer, Michael Sorkin, and Stanley Tigerman.

Recommendations

Annual Symposium

"Making the Case: Design in the Social Agenda" provided an open forum for discussing the issue of design and social activism. As an annual event, the symposium would create attention and establish the discussion at a national level.

Publication

The team outlined a book that would discuss the problem of design in areas of social need. The book would include transcripts from e-mail surveys and focus groups, as well as the presentation of research and proposals for change.

Education

Throughout the academic year, one of the most prominent topics of discussion was that of education. We continually heard from groups that one of the most promising ways to "make a difference" in the way that design is viewed is through education. Though the team was not able to outline a tailored proposal for a curriculum, we discussed that design should be part of the general curricula at all levels, from elementary school through higher education. Proposed, is an education that can generate a more design-educated populace and more tolerant, considerate designers.

Results

Throughout the year, the team struggled with ways to address those currently withheld good design—particularly in areas of social need. Not until the symposium did the team finally see that the discussion of design and social activism was something theorists, practitioners, design professionals and the general public not only were interested in, but were invested in. After grappling for months on how to define the topic, the symposium allowed an opportunity to bring together the issues at hand and place them on the public agenda.

THREE PROJECTS

THE CASE FOR GOOD DESIGN
A MANIFESTO

Jennifer Baker, Mary Davis, Sevra Davis, David Harrell, Christina Hoxie, Lyn Payton

We have been asleep too long! And while we slumber, innovation, invention and creativity lie on their deathbeds, infected with societal disregard. Where "necessity was [once] the mother of invention," speed and economics have pierced our society's fragile epidermis, racing through our veins and anesthetizing our collective soul into the naïve belief that without them, we will not survive.

This blatant social disrespect for the value of innovation, invention and creativity is a sign of the numbing and dumbing of our hurried culture. Our eyes and minds must be awakened to the importance of the creative nature that slips away in our rush to work. The ability to be a good, free-thinking, inventive society has disappeared along with a system of values, an awareness of humanity, and honesty and respectful interaction with others.

And thus we put forth this manifesto of good design: Let us leave behind the days of our muted shuffling in queue along the prefabricated path called success that our surrounding media advertises and prescribes to us. Let us leave behind the days where consumerism dictates what we value in the world and creativity is merely a catalyst for getting a product on the market sooner and for greater profit. We must push forth to a new age where creativity has a value greater than exchangeable commodities and will thus be given its rightful opportunity to benefit all individuals, communities and societies. We believe in the power of creativity and the result that is good design to enrich the lives of all those who encounter it. And so we will fight for the fair distribution of good design to all, regardless of race, age, sex, income, religion, education, or physical and mental health and ability. We will not tolerate the deeming of any individual or larger section of society unworthy or undeserving; and above all, we will promote a universal respect for one another through the fair dissemination of good design.

Blinded by the consumeristic direction of the current free-market based capitalist American society, design has come to be understood only as a tangible and marketable product. We believe that design is a process, of which a tangible product is only one result. We do not deny that architecture, industrial design, graphic design, Web design and a host of other tangible products are crucial to the visual development of design, but we must broaden our definition if we are to move forward and to better understand the compelling effect that design can have on us and our surroundings.

The process of design should engage the culture and society in which it is produced and from the resources that exist there, with the goal of providing an appropriate and necessary addition to the welfare of the individual and the larger social, economic and

306090 03 09 | 02

environmental community to which it belongs. Good design seeks solutions to the needs of a community in its own context and utilizes community resources to come to fruition. The criteria for measuring the value of design are: aesthetics, function, accessibility, appropriateness/context, durability, efficiency, quality, thoughtfulness, value, and ethics. Good design addresses and provides innovative solutions to the challenges we face in daily life—great and small. Good design eliminates obstacles or renders them unnoticeable. Good design seeks global rather than localized application. Good design works.

Good design is often confused with subjective beauty. In order to truly understand design, we must first separate the concept of aesthetic appeal from design. Far too often in design—particularly in architecture—acclaim is based solely on image. While there are practical reasons for focusing on appearance—and aesthetics are an undeniably important component of design—the consequence is that the success of a design is mistakenly judged not on whether it meets functional requirements, but its facade. Moreover, aesthetics is inherently subjective.

Today we are a culture of lemmings running after the latest trends in fashion, cuisine, home furnishings, art, architecture and infinite other goods. We are all too ready to accept the ready-made-tract-home mentality than apply our own judgment toward progressing our community and culture.

Our society has lost the ability to create intuitively. Certainly people are hired to create, where invention is tied to livelihood, but because of capitalism and the inundation of marketed products, we've primarily turned our minds off to making decisions about how we can impact our own surroundings and lifestyle because advertisements tell us how to live. We have lost the impulse to invent simply because of a perceived lack of necessity. And, though it would be difficult to argue that Americans in the early twenty-first century require anything more than we have, it is precisely because we have too much that our only impulse is to consume rather than think, create and invent. The ability and power to revise our life and culture allows us the hope to continually improve.

Because of this dearth of creativity and necessity, it is only the well-off who demand good design because it is expected in our socio-economic system. As a result, the vulnerable are left behind. Good and bad design cuts through all sections of our society, from rich to poor. Yet the wealthy are far more immune to the effects of bad design. They might purchase poorly constructed condominiums and suburban mansions, but they have the choice to buy something else. Other segments of society—who are not so fortunate—lack choices and are far more likely to be saddled with bad design.

This inequitable distribution of good design exists for a number of reasons, ranging from benign neglect, such as the lack of thought that caused the designers of O'Hare airport to make the restroom entrances too narrow to allow the passage of luggage-carrying travelers, to examples of overt racism and discrimination. Such examples include the post-War mentality of the 1950s and 1960s in Chicago that resulted in public housing for minorities intentionally designed to keep minorities isolated and segregated from the city. Selfishness and value engineering are also examples of how this situation can be perpetuated, like the developer who knowingly reduces the insulation in a building to save money and turn a greater profit.

Collectively, our society must accept responsibility for design successes and failures; the finger-pointing must stop: designers alone are not responsible for good and bad design. In thinking of design as a process, it is also necessary to understand that the process involves a number of different individuals, resources and ideas. Therefore, the collective should be held accountable and accept responsibility for design successes and failures.

Promoting the fair dissemination of good design is a difficult task, but one which we gladly tackle in the interest of establishing an atmosphere of respect for each other and for the power of design. Yet we realize that a manifesto in our current day would be naive to embrace the great optimism of past movements. And though the tone of this declaration may be more reserved than those in history, we approach this manifesto with prudence and caution, but with no less hope or idealism than those of our predecessors.

We call for the education, recognition, and promotion of good design for all sections of our society, particularly in the areas that are already underserved and underfunded, for it is there where innovation will have the greatest benefit and impact. We will strive to uphold the ethical component of design, in terms of the resources and materials used, and its impact on the physical and societal environment. We endorse the intrinsic value of good design and believe that good design can have a positive impact on individuals, communities, and our society as a whole. Ultimately, we will promote a public awareness of the universal respect for one another through the fair dissemination of good design to all.

pp. 80-89 "Three Projects" ©2002 Archeworks, Published by 306090, Inc.

THE PATH TO KAHN

Nathaniel Kahn's struggle to tell the story of his father Louis I. Kahn presents a new paradigm for history in the filmic context

by Melissa Gronlund

306090 03 09 02

pp. 90-97 "The Path to Kahn" ©2002 Melissa Gronlund, Published by 306090, Inc.

Every discipline has its genius figure—art its van Gogh, philosophy its Nietzsche, music its Mozart— the artist whose level of brilliance is matched only by his or her unease in daily life, and perhaps by the number of biographies written, filmed or otherwise made about them. In architecture, Louis Kahn should seem perfect for the role of uncompromising genius, yet his public persona, full of contradictions, complexities and ironies, has proved enduringly frustrating to nail down in architectural history.

That might change with renewed interest in his works and the upcoming documentary *KAHN*, directed by his son, Nathaniel Kahn. Through interviews and tours of Kahn's works, the film sketches the famous character of Louis Kahn: the spirituality, the aphorisms, and the profound love of architecture. And, while tracing the architect and his buildings, *KAHN* also seeks to find the man—in this case, the father—behind the architect.

KAHN will be released in film festivals this winter, holding its own among indie films with an appealing mix of architectural history—a field that has recently suffered neglect in deference to architectural theory—and the Oprah-esque journey of a son's search for his father. Nathaniel, who was only a boy when Kahn died, and who never knew him much while he was alive, frames the film as a personal journey to discover his absent father—an angle as

Melissa Gronlund is an editor of 306090.

Nathaniel meets Phillip Johnson >

< Interview with Vincent Scully

strangely universal, and even generic for a child of a workaholic parent. The emotional basis of the film is by no means simple, however. While inviting us to see Kahn as any other father, not letting him get away with his absence simply because of what he was producing at the studio, the film also emphatically details what an exceptional man Kahn was, and advocates the redemptive view of Kahn as an artist. Love and admiration motivate the film; but also resentment and anger.

KAHN begins at the end, with Kahn's death in 1974 in New York's Pennsylvania Station, when he collapsed of a heart attack in the men's bathroom on his way home from overseeing the construction of the business school in Ahmedabad, India. As the only card in his wallet listed his office address, he lay unidentified for three days while city workers tried to reach his studio. The irony of the circumstances—for an architect to die in Penn Station, one of the great architectural losses of the last century—and the poignancy of Kahn's lying anonymous, despite his fame in architectural circles and the public importance of his work, make for a gripping start and a powerful image for the film. *KAHN* suggests that architectural history has yet to settle on a place for Kahn—he is, in some way, still waiting to be identified.

Nathaniel, who narrates the film, created *KAHN* along with Simon Egleton and Susan Behr. The documentary takes the viewer through Kahn's life and work—which some might argue were the same—from Philadelphia to Jerusalem, La Jolla to Bangladesh. Nathaniel interviews figures ranging from a taxi driver who often drove Kahn home from his studio (Kahn, he says, always sat in the front seat), to architects like Frank Gehry, Philip Johnson, and I. M. Pei. Kahn's buildings serve as backdrops for the interviews, while also serving as subjects themselves—recalling Kahn's famous remark that you are a different person if you shower in a room with a 50-foot ceiling. "In the same way," Nathaniel observes, "people say different things. Maybe they're inspired."

The film shows archival footage of Kahn, teaching a seminar at the University of Pennsylvania, for instance, or walking through the construction of the Kimbell Museum of Art in Fort Worth, Texas. In addition to the major buildings, it also shows lesser-known works like a metal concert barge that Kahn built in the 1960s, which carries an orchestra from town to town along the New England coastline. Best of all are the shots of Dhaka.

If Nathaniel Kahn lets the work tell the story of the man, he shows every willingness to let the story of the man reflect the work as well. Louis Kahn was born on the island of Saaremaa, Estonia, probably in 1901, to a Latvian mother and an Estonian father.

They immigrated to the United States in 1906, settling in Philadelphia, where Kahn would live, study (at the University of Pennsylvania), and have his studio for the rest of his life. He had three children with three different women: In 1930 he married Esther Israeli, with whom he had a daughter, Sue Ann. He had another daughter, Alexandra Tyng, with the architect Anne Tyng, and with Harriet Pattison, at the age of 61, Nathaniel.

Kahn would return to Estonia in 1928, on a trip that brought him through England, the Netherlands, Germany, Scandinavia, and Italy. This trip exposed him to the modernist style that marks his early works. His second trip to Europe, on an American Academy in Rome fellowship from 1950–51, is generally regarded as seminal for his later, trademark works of heavy monumentality and geometric compositions. (In the documentary, Kahn's own sketches and watercolors of Greco-Roman and Egyptian structures, made during the trip, illustrate this episode.)

Kahn set himself apart from modernism with his first commission, for the Yale University Art Gallery (1951–53), as it emphasized geometric order, which at the time ran contrary to modernism's ideal of spatial continuity. If he was a misfit in modernism, Kahn was an outcast in postmodernism, with its intellectualized pastiche of the historical sources he regarded as essential. With postmodernism's decline, accordingly, Kahn's works have gained a more widespread popularity. Terrence Riley, senior curator of architecture and design at New York's Museum of Modern Art, says,

> There was a retrospective about ten years ago at LAMOCA that was a little too early. For the Kahn devotees, it was like preaching to the converted. For the rest, there was still a hangover from postmodernism, from that thrill of deconstruction. Lately, though, we've been in this millennium bubble, with an emphasis on the future with a capital *F*—a kind of reaction to post modernism. People are looking more seriously at architecture.

Kahn stands for many as the antithesis of the 1980s movement. In the film, for instance, Frank Gehry provides a great off-the-cuff, succinct explanation of the transition from modernism to postmodernism, and of Kahn's role in bringing original expression back to the forefront. "Architecture got passionless and mechanical," he says. "The postmodernist thing happened because people couldn't handle it. … My first works came out of reverence for Kahn." That Gehry—who many see as responsible for popularizing the notion of architect-as-artist in the 90s—identifies Kahn as the influence for his move towards a distinctive style is ironic, considering how little the current trend has in common with the perception of

pp. 90–97 "The Path to Kahn" ©2002 Melissa Gronlund, Published by 306090, Inc.

< Government Complex in Bangladesh >

< Interview with Frank O Gehry >

Kahn as an artist, but not surprising. What is most apparent after watching *KAHN* or reading works on him written by contemporaries is the ubiquity and consistency of the view of Kahn as an artist, even to the point of suggesting that his genius is divinely inspired.

This understanding of Kahn is also crucial to the film's take on Kahn's canonization. Nathaniel cites one image as epitomizing his father: Kahn in his studio with charcoal on his hands. "He's absolutely, fundamentally an artist," Nathaniel says, "I'm trying to show him as an artist … the price that he paid and the price others paid." The rationale, perhaps, is that if Kahn is an artist, he is somehow absolved of the guilt for the hurt he inflicted on others—that his transcendent works elevate him beyond the plane of everyday matters. In one of *KAHN's* interviews, Vincent Scully, professor emeritus of art history at Yale and a former colleague of Kahn's, relates the idea that in Jewish mysticism, the Jewish God manifests Himself through His works on earth. Though Nathaniel argues that in his later years, Kahn played up this image, adding "mumbo jumbo to the mix." People invariably use religious words to describe him: messianic, mystic, holy, inspired. In Scully's introduction to the exhibition catalog (published by Rizzoli) for "Louis I. Kahn: In the Realm of Architecture," the retrospective organized by the Los Angeles Museum of Contemporary Art in the early 1990s, he writes that Kahn's works "thrum with silence, as with the presence of God," and that Kahn himself recalls soulful Russian writers like Tolstoy, Gorky, or Dostoevsky. The image is fully fleshed out, from his physical characteristics—the piercing blue eyes, the face scarred from childhood disease—to his manner of speaking: "What does a brick want to be? A brick." Fascinated with the ruins of the past, we read in him an inability to reconcile with the present.

This image of Kahn as an artist differs fundamentally from the current trend of seeing architecture as art—a perception that has its origins more in the cultural landscape than in the architects themselves, and which rests on concepts not frequently associated with Kahn, like accessibility and media showmanship. Riley notes that

> Kahn wasn't charismatic in the media sense—he wasn't that good looking, not the life of the party. There's this famous television clip with him and Philip Johnson where Johnson ties him in knots. Kahn's a little too earnest, a little too serious. But he attracts these followers who are totally devoted.

The Guggenheim Bilbao is generally seen as the pinnacle of both the starchitect trend and the labeling of buildings as sculpture. The Guggenheim Museum self-referentially refers to Gehry's buildings as "pow-

erful essays in primal geometric forms"—a description that seems tailor-made for Kahn but is more publicly apparent in Gehry's accessible and dramatic work. The view also has a lot to do with the American skepticism of the intellectual elite. With much of contemporary art often perceived as incomprehensible, architecture has emerged as the populist antidote—in the public realm by definition, and deliberately accessible as of late.

The two disciplines have recently grown closer together. Barbara MacAdam, senior editor of *ARTnews*, explains:

> Architecture has followed some of the formal—and less so-trends in art and looks similar to a lot of sculpture. In fact, the two art forms are highly compatible. Witness, most obviously, Serra and Gehry. Artists and architects have also been collaborating on projects for quite a while. Gehry, again, worked with Oldenburg on his Disney Project in L.A. … And the computer has allowed architects a different, freer way of rendering, which also permits more 'art'-like forms.

The current practice of exhibiting preparatory materials and sketches in museums and galleries, notes MacAdam, has added to the merging of the two disciplines. In the summer of 2001, there were three architecture retrospectives in New York (two on Mies, at the Whitney and the Modern, and one at the Guggenheim on Gehry), and the Philadelphia Museum of Art showed the work of Robert Venturi and Denise Scott Brown. Galleries have also grown larger, making them more amenable, MacAdam says, to showing architectural projects and early renderings. Importantly, however, Riley remarks that "Kahn's drawings are not very interesting compared to Mies' or Gehry's or Venturi's. His work was really in the architecture."

Riley insists that architecture is different than art, and bristles at the conflation of the two.

> If someone is a really good architect, then they make really good architecture. The comparison somehow implies that a great architect has somehow graduated to being an artist, when the two disciplines deal with different ethics… Kahn understood building not as a sculpture, but as a process. The whole idea of served and servant spaces—there was no behind-the-scenes for him. That's the mark of a real architect: his concern with things out of the public eye. If you go into one of his bathrooms, they're like chapels.

Of course, it is Kahn's focus on the essence of architecture that many cite as, indeed, elevating him to the plane of art.

306090 03 09 | 02

Salk Institute

pp. 90-97 "The Path to Kahn" ©2002 Melissa Gronlund, Published by 306090, Inc.

KAHN, meanwhile, demonstrates that the medium of film is expertly suited for architecture. Both media create an experience that is not in control of the participant: film dictates what is seen and when, just as architecture determines movement through a space. Like Iñigo Manglano-Ovalle's superb time-elapsed video (*Alltagszeit*, 2001) of 12 hours in Mies' Berlin Neue Nationalgalerie, Nathaniel uses time-elapsed photography to reveal the passage of time. The technique particularly shows off Kahn's masterful use of natural light: the sun sinking into the courtyard of the Salk Institute, or the darkening of the Kimbell museum as clouds pass overhead. Viewed in time-elapse, the buildings evoke an unsettling sense of evanescence. "Often," Nathaniel said, "I felt up against the strong feeling that humans persist for a lot shorter time than buildings." This is heightened by the fact that Kahn's buildings, inspired by the relics of Egypt and Rome, already resemble ruins. In the war of partition between West Pakistan (present-day Pakistan) and East Pakistan (Bangladesh) in 1971, according to Nathaniel, the Pakistanis did not bomb Kahn's Bangladesh complex because they mistook it for ancient ruins. Kahn's masterpiece was literally saved by its own rough-hewn and monumental aesthetic.

The film ends on this complex, built in Sher-e-Bangla Nagar, Dhaka, from 1962 to 1983 as the second capital of divided Pakistan. The project had first been offered to Le Corbusier, who was too busy and turned it down, and Alvar Aalto, who was sick at the time. The buildings resemble a small city, with an assembly hall, a prayer hall, and hostels located along a main axis. By the time it was completed, Kahn had been dead for nine years, and it served as the capital of a new nation, Bangladesh.

Notably, Kahn's largest and most ambitious project is in South Asia, a region far removed from the Western canon. It is the ultimate test of a building—out in the middle of Western-architectural nowhere, where terms like self-referentiality and pastiche are meaningless. The cult of the architect is also taken down superbly. Nathaniel approaches a group of Bangladeshi men, explaining that he is making a documentary about the architect of the complex. "He's my father," Nathaniel says proudly, asking them if they know his name. "Louis…" he prompts them. On cue, one offers: "Farrakhan!"

In ending on Dhaka, Nathaniel quite consciously fulfills the journey that his father was never able to finish. His pride in the building is clear. In an interview with Shamsul Wares, the Bangladeshi architecture professor, he speaks about how Kahn is "a real artist," how sacrificed his family for his art and for the people of Bangladesh. "He gave us the institution for democracy. We are the poorest country, and he paid his life for this." It is the age-old trade-off of loving humanity but not individuals, of giving up yourself for your art.

Nathaniel's tribute to his father neither romanticizes nor mythologizes him—a hard task to accomplish when dealing with the personage of Kahn, who seemed to fashion what he said as well as what he built with an eye to posterity. This, though, is exactly the reason Kahn should be remembered and revered: for his deep commitment to architecture. During a lecture in Philadelphia at the Drexler Architectural Society in 1968, he said, "You realize when you are in the realm of architecture that you are touching the basic feelings of man, and that architecture would never have been part of humanity if it weren't the truth to begin with." It is a belief in a practice that transcends movements and ages, and even the buildings we create.

pp. 90–97 "The Path to Kahn" ©2002 Melissa Gronlund, Published by 306090, Inc.

Center Library

For their generous contributions,
306090 wishes to thank:

The Graham Foundation for Advanced Studies in the Fine Arts

and

The School of Architecture, Princeton University
The Hillier Group
The Michael Sorkin Studio

M. Christine Boyer
Beatriz Colomina
Claire Flom
Leslie and Peter Flom
Jason and Wendy Flom
David L Hays
Allen R. Kramer
Anne R. Kreeger
Nancy Laing
Kevin Lippert
Richard Solomon

306090 would also like to thank:

Joseph and Sharon Abruzzo, Nettie Aljian, Karen Begley, Melissa
Bermudez, Penny Chu, Henry N. Cobb, Simon Egleton, Nancy Laing,
Lewis.Tsurumaki.Lewis and the Essex Street Studios, Kevin Lippert,
Vram Malek, Scott G. Paterson, Yuki Sakamoto, Stanley Tigerman
and Ronald Weiss.

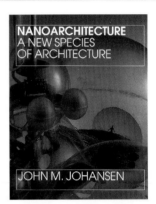
Advertisements

FREECELL

contact   718 643 4180   www.frcll.com
35 YORK ST   UNIT 1109   BROOKLYN NY 11201

TRACTOR CHAIR>>>FLIP-SIDE COFFEE TABLE>>>ROLLING OFFICE PARTITION>>>SEAT STORAGE>>>SWING BALL
products

```
   ~MY AQUARIUM OF FISH~
~~~~~~~~~~~~~~~~~~~~~~~~~~~~~~~~~~~~~~~~~~~~~~~~~~~~~~~~~~~~~~~~~~~~~~~~~~~
        .            `         /
                 .      ,../...            .
        .            .  /        `\  /   .
    \    .       o          < ' )     =<
    /\  .                  \ \      /  \       .    __
  >=)'>                     `'\'"'"'          /o \/
    \/  .    /         o            /,         \__/\   .:/
    /   .  /--\ /          /        <')=<    .     ,,///;,   ,;/
        <o)  =<       . / \          \`        .   o:::::::;;///
         \_/ \       <')_=<           \_/           >::::::::;;\\\
           \              \_/           .           ''\\\\\''  ';\
  (                        \          __
   )                                 <'_><         (
  (         (                  ,/...                 )
   )    (      )            <')  `=<          )    (
  (       )  (            ``\```           (      )
____)____(___)_____)___(_____jgs_
(some of the fish in here are my creations, 3 are not...
 from left to right- yes is my original work, no is someone else's...
 yes, no, yes, yes/yes (tie), yes, yes, no, and no)
```

(abinet
A quarterly magazine of art and culture

Ⓞ Published by Immaterial Incorporated
See www.immaterial.net/cabinet for further information

ay, ny

306090

mg, ny

cs, ny

ea, nj   js, nj   jw, dc   ab, ny

Donations Form # S-4 2002-3 306090 Inc. of New Jersey USA
@ 2002 306090, inc. Please fill out this form in its entirety.
Do not photocopy!

donate. 306090

306090 is committed to bringing you the most important
new developments by students and young professionals in
architecture and design. As a non-profit, volunteer effort,
306090 relies entirely on donations for support of its production. Sponsorship is welcomed at all levels. Contributions are
tax-deduct able. Help support the future of architecture.

Fill out this form:

I am an: ☐ individual ☐ organization ☐ institution

I would like to support the future of architecture
with a tax-exempt contribution to 306090 of:

$ _____ .oo

☐☐☐☐☐☐☐☐☐☐☐☐☐☐☐☐☐☐☐
Name

M M / D D / Y Y   ☐☐☐
dob   Blood Type

(in name of): _____

☐☐☐☐☐☐☐☐☐☐☐☐☐☐☐☐☐☐☐☐
e-mail

Address: _____

**! donate on-line using your credit card
through justgive.org at 306090.org !**

Avoid long lines at inspection stations, remit this form and any inquiries to:

306090, Inc.   www.306090.org
35A Park Pl.   info@306090.org
Princeton, NJ 08542

signature: _____   date: _____

306090, A Journal of Emergent Architecture and Design, was
organized in 2001 by students at the School of Architecture,
Princeton University, and has since enveloped a widening
band of writers, architects and designers from across the
country. The mission of the journal, published biannually,
is to reinvigorate the current architectural discipline by
introducing and recognizing the work of promising students and
young professionals whose cross-disciplinary projects, ideas,
buildings, and other media offer innovative directions for
the growth of architecture. It is the intent of this journal
to consistently reposition the work of students and young
professionals into the cross hairs of the present architectural
discourse.

306090 is unique in that it is seeking specifically to publish
ideologically and geographically diverse work and to directly
address issues of education, practice and politics. 306090 is a
resource for exposing projects and positions that are untested,
unforeseen, unabashed and vital. Proposed as an alternative
to current academic and commercial publications, 306090 is
dedicated to the exposure of the work of architecture students
and young design professionals whose active engagement in the
theorizing and experimentation of architecture and aesthetic
practices will guide the future of the discipline.

Education Form # S-4 2002-3 306090 Inc. of New Jersey USA
@ 2002 306090, inc. Please fill out this form in its entirety.
Do not photocopy!

Call for Submissions Form # S-4 2002-3 306090 Inc. of New Jersey, USA
© 2002 306090, inc. Please fill out this form in its entirety.
Do not photocopy!

submit. 306090

306090 wishes to publish politically charged articles
and projects that defy contemporary norms. We encourage
articles of a controversial nature, articles which challenge
the academic, cultural and professional institution of
architecture. We accept articles and projects from students,
from professors and faculty, and from young professionals.
We attempt to publish work that has not been published
elsewhere. We attempt to publish ideas that are fresh and
inspiring. If you have a project or text that you think
would be appropriate for this journal, please contact us
using this form.

☐ I am submitting work
for:
306090 04
DEADLINE: 30 NOV 2002

☐ I am submitting work
for:
306090 05
DEADLINE: 30 MAY 2003

Name

M M / D D / Y Y   (☐☐☐) ☐☐☐☐☐☐☐
dob   telephone

Project Title: _____

E-mail:

Website: ☐ Please add my website to the links page of www.306090.org
Address: _____

In case of emergency, contact: _____

Biographical statement: _____

Project title: _____

Attachment checklist:
(note: you must submit these items with your form by the above deadline. Attachment must be
made in digital form on a PC readable disk. Please include a stamped, self-addressed envelope,
otherwise 306090 cannot be responsible for returning these attachments. Contact 306090 at the
address above with any questions.)

☐ all text *.txt   ☐ all image files   ☐ all vector   ☐ all included
or *.doc format   in 300 dpi   files in pro-   on pc formatted
                     greyscale   cess black   zip or compact
                     *.tif format   *.eps format   disk

signature: _____ date: _____

! Avoid undue charges ! Address this form promptly to:

306090, Operations
59 Jefferson St. #404
Brooklyn, NY 11206

www.306090.org
info@306090.org

306090 is proud to be distributed by Princeton Architectural
Press. Orders can be placed online at www.papress.com or by
contacting: Princeton Architectural Press 37 East 7th Street
New York, New York 10003 (800) 722-6657. 306090 is also
available through amazon.com, bn.com, chroniclebooks.com, and
architectural bookstores worldwide.

Disseminations Form # S-4 2002-3 306090 Inc. of New Jersey USA
© 2002 306090, inc. Please fill out this form in its entirety.
Do not photocopy!